D1245392

Anthony Perkins, Connie Stevens and Richard Benjamin in a scene from the New York production of "The Star-Spangled Girl." Set designed by Oliver Smith.

THE
STAR-SPANGLED
GIRL

BY NEIL SIMON

★

A NEW COMEDY

★

DRAMATISTS
PLAY SERVICE
INC.

SOUND EFFECTS

The following is a list of sound effects referenced in this play:

Typewriter
Telephone bell, door bell

THE STAR-SPANGLED GIRL was first presented by Saint-Subber at the Plymouth Theatre, in New York City, on December 21, 1966. It was directed by George Axelrod; scenic production was by Oliver Smith; lighting was by Jean Rosenthal; and the costumes were by Ann Roth. The cast, is order of appearance, was as follows:

ANDY HOBART .... Anthony Perkins

NORMAN CORNELL .... Richard Benjamin

SOPHIE RAUSCHMEYER .... Connie Stevens

SYNOPSIS OF SCENES

A duplex studio apartment in San Francisco.

ACT I

Scene 1: It's late afternoon, early summer.

Scene 2: Three days later.

ACT II

Scene 1: The next day. About 5 P.M.

Scene 2: A few days later.

ACT III

The next day. Early afternoon.

THE
STAR-SPANGLED GIRL

ACT I

SCENE 1

A duplex studio apartment overlooking the bay in San Francisco. It's not as nice as it sounds. It's a wood shingled building about fifty years old. It was probably once the large Victorian home of a wealthy family and in due course fell to its present state, an apartment and furnished room multiple dwelling. Still, it's not without its charm.

The apartment is shared by two young men, Andy Hobart and Norman Cornell. However, at first glance, one can see that their "home" has a double function. It also serves as their place of business, the offices of their small magazine, Fallout.

On the first level (stage floor): The entrance to the apartment is up center, at the top of three stairs. Up right center is a long kitchen bar, or counter, on which we see a tall vase holding a feather duster, a lamp, a ukulele, an apothecary jar with candy and a potted vine. The shelves underneath hold an assortment of glasses, bottles, books and old magazines. Upstage of the counter in a small alcove is a door leading to a closet. To the right of the closet door is an open doorway leading to their kitchen. On the wall, left of the closet, is a set of shelves filled with cans of beans.

On the stage left wall is a window with a match-stick blind. Near the window is a pipe running from the floor through a small table to the skylight. Down left, parallel to the footlights, is a six-foot table on which we see a tape recorder, an old portable typewriter, a goose neck lamp, a stack of yellow paper, a pile of envelopes, news-

paper clippings held together with a large paper clip, a dummy or mock-up copy of Fallout, a container for a roll of stamps, erasers, etc. A straight wooden chair is upstage of the desk, a wastebasket to the left. Under the left end of the desk is a pile of back issues of Fallout. On the left wall, downstage of the window, is a bulletin board. "A Remedy for a Sick Society" is a sign near the top. The remainder of the board is covered with clippings, pictures, notes and a small mirror. Below the board is a slant top desk, on which rests a large dictionary, a magazine and a pipe. There are two drawers in this desk. The telephone with push buttons, and a stack of magazines are on the pole table. Under the same table is a pile of old magazines and a bundle of old papers tied together. In the up left corner is a large bulletin board, below which is a small table filled with a supply of yellow paper, a cup holding pens and pencils, stapler, clip-board, empty apothecary jar, empty beer cans, etc. Under the table is a bundle of old paper and an old gallon can of green paint with a brush and stirrer inside. To the table's right is a small radiator. On top of the radiator is a board, making space for an electric pencil sharpener and a pair of scissors. Downstage of the radiator is a pile of newspapers tied in a bundle, with a cardboard carton on top. To the right is a small wooden stool.

In the center of the stage is a low round table, the base is made of two car tires. On the table: newspaper, magazines, ashtray, mug with pencils, coffee pot, plate with crumbs, dirty coffee cup, empty jam jar and a stamp pad with a rubber stamp. To the left of the table is a director's chair, to the right, a wooden chair. Down right, a sofa—no back—runs parallel with the footlights. At the right end of the sofa is a table with magazines, books, a goose neck lamp, ashtray, dumbbell, old alarm clock, empty box of cookies, etc. Another section of the sofa follows the right wall upstage extending under a landing and the flight of stairs to the landing. Pillows are scattered on this section of the sofa. On the down right wall, above sofa, is a shelf holding books, magazines and three

6

milk bottles filled with pennies. Above the shelf on the wall is another cluttered bulletin board.

Next to the stairs, leading to the landing, is a rattan hassock, with a stack of newspapers and an empty beer can on top. Upstage of the steps is a high stool—next to kitchen bar.

On the landing, the first level off the floor, is a large telescope pointing through a bay window on the right wall. No shades or curtains on this window. A light fixture with two bare light bulbs is downstage. Bookcases and shelves, filled with books and an occasional plant, take up the remaining wall space on the landing.

Four steps from the upstage end of the landing lead to the balcony where there are three doors, the right one is Andy's, the one on the wall facing the audience is Norman's and the third one is a small door, reached by a short ladder, leading to the roof.

It's late afternoon. Early summer.

The door opens and Andy Hobart enters. He is about 26, but has the worried look of a man twice his age. Andy is a dedicated, idealistic cynic charged with the energy of an angry generation. He wears an old tan sport jacket over his khaki trousers, a checked shirt and no tie. He carries a briefcase that has seen better days. As he enters he looks over at the desk and seems amazed and annoyed not to see someone there.

ANDY. Norman? . . . You home? I take it by your silence that you're not home . . . (*Crosses to tape recorder on desk.*) So where are you? (*He turns machine on. Puts briefcase down.*)
NORMAN'S VOICE. I'm up on the roof stealing laundry . . . You may be wearing a pink housecoat tomorrow, but at least it'll be clean . . . How about those finished pages on the desk? (*Andy picks them up and looks through them.*) . . . I've been pounding the typewriter for nine straight hours. I am now capable of committing the perfect crime because I no longer have fingerprints . . . Mr. Franklyn telephoned five times. I repeat, five times . . . He said we owe him six hundred dollars in printing bills and fifty cents for five telephone calls . . . He also said if he doesn't get his money by Saturday, he's going to send over

his two sons to break our four legs . . . I told him, "I'm just a writer and *you* take care of all bills," so they're going to break your legs and just sprain my ankle . . . I am now finished talking so please turn me off. (*Andy turns off tape as the telephone rings. He answers it.*)

ANDY. *Fallout* magazine . . . Who's calling, please? . . . Mr. Franklyn . . . One moment, Mr. Franklyn, I'll give you our billing department . . . (*He presses button and uses Titus Moody voice. Sits on the pole table.*) . . . Billing department . . . Yes? . . . Oh, Mr. Franklyn . . . Yes, I got your five messages . . . You mean you haven't received our check? . . . I can't understand that . . . Why just yesterday . . . (*He presses down on receiver and cuts off call. He looks over Norman's pages. The telephone rings again. He picks it up.*) *Fallout* magazine . . . Oh, Mr. Franklyn, I guess you got cut off. Sorry. I'll give you our billing department. (*He presses button and resumes Titus Moody voice. Sits.*) Billing department . . . Oh, yes, Mr. Franklyn. Well— (*Again he deliberately clicks off. He hangs up and waits. The phone rings again. Andy uses the nasal voice of a telephone operator.*) . . . And a fifty percent chance of showers today. Tomorrow morning—clearing with patches of fog— (*He winces as Franklyn hangs up hard.*) I don't know what you're so sore about, Franklyn. You may not be getting your money, but at least you know it's going to rain. (*The telephone rings again. Andy turns on the tape machine and records.*) . . . Hey, Luigi, how about a little service? (*The telephone rings again and he records that too. He turns off machine and picks up phone and takes it to the desk.*) . . . Luigi's Restaurant . . . Who? . . . No, is no magazine. Is Luigi's Restaurant . . . (*He turns on tape and plays back*)

ANDY'S VOICE. Hey, Luigi, how about a little service?

ANDY. Si, si, I'm a coming. (*The phone rings on tape recorder.*) 'Scusa, my other phone, she's a ringing. (*He hangs up and rubs his hands with satisfaction.*) I can keep this up as long as you can, Franklyn. (*The roof door opens and Norman comes down the ladder carrying a basket of laundry. Norman is about the same age as Andy. Although he is the Brain, the intellect behind Fallout, when he is away from the typewriter, he is an incorrigible adolescent.*)

8

NORMAN. (On 'balcony.) I just saved us eight dollars in laundry bills. And I found you your blue shirt.

ANDY. I didn't lose one.

NORMAN. I didn't say you did. I just said I found you one.

ANDY. Did you have lunch today?

NORMAN. (Comes down steps to landing.) Certainly. I had one sardine on a frozen waffle.

ANDY. Why?

NORMAN. Because that's all there was.

ANDY. You mean there's nothing else to eat in the refrigerator?

NORMAN. There's three ice cubes and a light bulb. I'm saving them for tomorrow. (At the center table, he puts basket down. Then he holds up a shirt.) I'll put this in the freezer. We don't have any more starch. (He takes shirt into kitchen.)

ANDY. (Sits on the pole table.) Norman, it's just occurred to me that being poor is very boring. We really wouldn't have to worry about money if you would let me do what I suggested.

NORMAN. (Comes out of kitchen and goes down right to table between sofas.) What was that?

ANDY. Selling you to a medical school.

NORMAN. Never mind me, how about selling the magazine? How'd you do today?

ANDY. If selling two subscriptions is good, we only did fair. (Norman picks up empty box of cookies.) Somehow I don't think the average San Francisco housewife is ready for a politically controversial magazine that is definitely anti-American . . . Is there any mail?

NORMAN. (Throws down the empty box.) In the wastebasket . . . (Goes to c. table.) I'm so hungry. (Puts clothes basket on floor, downstage of the L. chair. Eats crumbs from a plate on the table.)

ANDY. (Picks up wastebasket, puts it on pole table and goes through the bills.) Printing bills, typewriter repair bills, rent bills, electric bills, food bills, gas bills. This is a bill for the waste paper basket.

NORMAN. (Running his finger around the empty jam jar in search of food.) And we owe the lady from the pet shop eighty cents.

ANDY. The pet shop? What for?

NORMAN. She gave me a haircut today.

ANDY. (*Returns wastebasket to* L. *of desk.*) Let me worry about the bills, Norman, you write the magazine. I need your blue jacket. I've got to go out tonight. (*Goes* U. L. *and gets blue jacket hanging* U. *of bulletin board.*)

NORMAN. Business?

ANDY. Why else would I do the Monkee until three o'clock in the morning at the Velvet Cucumber?

NORMAN. Who are you going with?

ANDY. Who do I go with every night? Our landlady, Mrs. Mackininee. (*Takes jacket* D. R. *to the sofa, where he lifts up the top mattress and lays the jacket between the mattress and springs. Drops the mattress down. Norman looks for food in the drawers of the slant-top desk.*) Norman, you have no idea what I go through to keep us from being thrown out on the street. (*Andy kneels on top of mattress. Puts all his weight on it—to press suit.*) Not only is she totally lacking in rhythm, but she has no sense of direction. Last night she Watusied out the door and into the parking lot. (*Rises and gets dumbbell. Rolls it over the mattress.*)

NOMAN. (*Good-naturedly at slant top desk, eating from a small cereal box he has found.*) It'll go down as one of the great sacrifices in journalistic history.

ANDY. You don't think it's humiliating to sit in a night club with a dark haired widow who wears blonde braids and picks up the bill?

NORMAN. She likes you, doesn't she? Why don't you take her to the beach for the weekend so we can have the apartment painted? (*Sits at desk.*)

ANDY. You think I want to fall off her motorcycle the way her husband did?

NORMAN. Listen, anytime you want to change places I'm perfectly willing. (*The telephone rings. Norman rises hurriedly and motions to Andy to answer it as he goes to the chair* L. *of the* C. *table. Sits and begins to fold clean socks. Andy crosses* L., *above the table, to answer the phone.*)

ANDY. (*Into phone, Titus Moody voice.*) Billing department! . . . (*Changes to his normal voice.*) Oh, Mrs. Mackininee . . . No, no, I wasn't trying to sound older. I think I caught a cold last night . . . Yes, on the back of the motorcycle . . . You really are a wonderful driver . . . Did you ever find your other braid? . . . Oh, too bad . . . I feel kind of responsible . . . Well, I do . . . I mean I felt myself slipping off and it was the first thing I grabbed . . . Yes, I'll pick you up at eight o'clock . . . Oh, that sounds wonderful. I can't wait to see them. Bye.

NORMAN. You can't wait to see what?

ANDY. Her new gold-sequined goggles . . . You can imagine how they look with her silver lamé jump suit . . . Promise me one thing.

NORMAN. What?

ANDY. If there's a crash and they find my body next to hers, tell my mother and father I was kidnapped. (*Andy goes* R. *and pulls suit from sofa and goes to the stairs with it.*)

NORMAN. Listen, when you come home tonight, I want to hear everything that happened. I don't care what time it is, wake me up and tell me.

ANDY. All right, Norman.

NORMAN. Don't say all right. Promise me. You'll wake me up and you'll tell me everything. Don't leave anything out.

ANDY. (*Leans over balcony. Looks at Norman with concern.*) Norman, I think you've been working too hard lately. Why don't you take the night off and go see a sexy movie?

NORMAN. How can I take the night off? We've got a magazine to get out here.

ANDY. You've got five days to finish three articles. You can do that with two fingers. Why don't you call up a girl?

NORMAN. You can't just call up a girl. You have to know her first.

ANDY. Well, call up a girl you know.

NORMAN. I don't like any of the girls I know. I only like the girls *you* know.

ANDY. All right, call up one of my girls.

NORMAN. I can't. I don't know them. (*Norman rises and takes clothes basket to kitchen. Returns and goes to desk.*)

ANDY. . . . Norman, I'm as dedicated to this magazine as you are. Maybe even more. You put your talent into it; I put in my blood. And it's my job to preserve that talent and keep it in perfect working order. That's why I want you to relax once in a while. If you don't, you're going to get a bubble on your head.

NORMAN. (*Seated at desk.*) I'll go out as soon as this issue is finished.

ANDY. Who will you go out with?

11

NORMAN. A beautiful, gorgeous blonde will move into the empty apartment next door and I'll fall madly in love. All right? ANDY. All right, Norman, if you're happier working, then I'm happy. Work all night and enjoy yourself. (*He goes into room and closes door. Norman sits at the typewriter and picks up clippings. He talks aloud to himself.*)

NORMAN. . . . I don't know how he expects me to finish a magazine if I don't sit down and finish it . . . Things do not get written by themselves . . . Unless he believes in elves and gnomes . . . And they don't write magazines, they repair shoes . . . (*He begins to type. The doorbell rings. He gets up, crosses to door and opens it. Sophie Rauschmeyer, a lovely young blonde, stands there. She is everything Norman has described. She is the prototype of the All-American girl. If she had a few freckles on her nose it would be perfect. Her compact, solid form and freshly scrubbed face tell us that this is a purely physical creature. What she can't do with an intellectual problem, she more than makes up for with her strong back-stroke or her straight back astride a horse. The Arkansas drawl doesn't add to her image as an intellect either. And best of all, she smells good.*)

SOPHIE. (*Big, warm smile.*) Excuse me. Mah name is Sophie Rauschmeyer. Ah just moved into the empty apartment next door . . . Ah know people in big cities don't usually do this, but ah promised mah folks ah would make mah akwaitance with mah neighbors so ah just want to say it's a pleasure meetin' you and hope ah see you again. Real soon. Bye! (*Big smile. She turns, closes door and goes. Norman has not flinched a muscle since she appeared. He now seems to be frozen to the spot and stands motionless for what seems to be an hour and a half.*)

ANDY. (*Comes out of his room, wearing blue jacket. No shoes.*) Did someone just ring the bell? . . . Norman, did someone just come in? (*Leans down and taps Norman on head.*)

NORMAN. What? What? (*Quickly.*) No! No! No one came in. There's no one here. Go back to your room.

ANDY. What's the matter, Norman?

NORMAN. There's nothing the matter. Leave me alone. Go back to your room. Can't you see I'm busy working?

ANDY. At the door?

NORMAN. I needed some air.

ANDY. Why don't you open the window?

12

NORMAN. I don't want fresh air. I want plain air . . . will you please go back to your room?

ANDY. All right, Norman. Don't tense up. Relax. Try and relax. (*He is about to go back into his room when the doorbell rings again. Andy stops and looks at Norman who doesn't move.*) . . . Now I hear a bell.

NORMAN. All right, so you hear a bell. People ring bells all day long. It's no reason for you to loiter on top of the stairs all night. (*The doorbell rings again.*)

ANDY. Are you going to answer that or am I?

NORMAN. I'm going to answer it. Stay up there. (*He looks at Andy hoping he'll go away. But he knows he won't so he opens the door. Sophie stands there again. She has a cake in her hands.*)

SOPHIE. (*Big smile.*) Excuse me again . . . Ah was just unpackin' and mah friends back home sent me this fruit cake with rum in it, which ah'm not allowed to eat 'cause ah'm in trainin' and ah'd hate to see it go to waste so ah'd appreciate it if you'd accept it with mah compliments. (*She gives him the cake.*) Nice seein' you again. Bye. (*She pulls door shut and exits. Norman gives a long look at the door.*)

ANDY. Who's that, Norman?

NORMAN. Never mind who it is, I saw her first.

ANDY. All right, you saw her first. Who is she?

NORMAN. (*Turns front.*) Her name is Sophie Rauschmeyer and she just moved into the empty apartment next door and she just gave me a fruit cake with rum in it and I love her. (*Running L., R. and all over the room.*) Wahoo! Did you see what moved into this building? Next door to where I live! (*Puts cake on pole table.*) It's for me. All for me. God loves me and He gave me something wonderful. (*Arms outstretched.*)

ANDY. (*Happy for Norman, on bottom step.*) I was going to get you one for Christmas.

NORMAN. (*He is now dancing all over the room.*) Did you smell her? Did you get one whiff of that fragrance? Did you open your entire nose and smell that girl?

ANDY. (*Comes down onto stage floor and goes L.*) I was upstairs, she didn't smell that far . . . I need your dancing shoes. (*Andy picks up the cake, gives it to Norman and then pushes him onto the pole table.*)

NORMAN. Didn't smell that far? It's all over the room. (*Andy*

13

pulls the director's chair L., *sits down and starts pulling off Norman's shoes.*) It's even out in the hall. I'll bet she's inundated the whole lousy neighborhood. They're gonna start raising rents. And you stay away from her.

ANDY. No contest. She's not my type.

NORMAN. Well, she's my type. (*Takes cake to kitchen—in stocking feet.*) How do you know what type she is?

ANDY. (*Pulls chair back to the* C. *table and gets rubber stamp.*) Norman, when it comes to girls, I have extra-sensory perception. (*He applies stamp to pad, then to the shoes.*) . . . She's the all-outdoor type. Enormously strong from the neck down.

NORMAN. (*Returns from kitchen. Goes to* R. *of* C. *table.*) Who cares what her I.Q. is? I'm not giving out any Fulbrights. I just want to smell her and touch her.

ANDY. All right. Go ring her doorbell and say you want to smell her and touch her.

NORMAN. Are you crazy, didn't you hear the way she talked? "Ah'm glad to make yo' akwaitance" . . . She comes from Rhett Butler country. The only way to make it with a girl like that is with romance, big gestures.

ANDY. All right. Go out and burn down Atlanta. She'll be crazy about you.

NORMAN. (*Going* L., D. *of table.*) You think I wouldn't do it if I could get to nibble on her chin for an hour?

ANDY. I was right. You've been working much too hard lately. (*Rises and goes* R. *to stairs.*)

NORMAN. (*Follows Andy.*) Wait a minute. Talk to me. (*Andy stops on stairs. Gets tie hanging on landing balustrade.*) Help me. I've got to plan this all very carefully. I mustn't jump into anything. One wrong move and I can blow the entire love affair . . . Flowers? What about flowers? Flowers every morning. Flowers twice a day . . . No. No. That's not big enough.

ANDY. (*Still on stairs. Puts on tie.*) How about trees?

NORMAN. Maybe it shouldn't be big. Maybe it should be small. Something with thought. Something personal. What could I do for her that's very small and very personal?

ANDY. How about brushing her teeth?

NORMAN. Get outa here! You're killing everything. You have no idea how to treat a girl like that.

ANDY. Personally I wouldn't try, but if she excites your nasal passages, Norman, I'm with you.

NORMAN. I got it! I got it! Where's the paint can? I need a can of green paint. (*Goes* L. *Gets paint can from under* L. *table.*)

ANDY. What are you going to do?

NORMAN. (*Goes to Andy.*) I'm going to paint the stairs. One letter on each step. So that when she comes home at night and goes up the stairs, it's going to read . . . (*He indicates with his finger going up the stairs.*) . . . I-love-you-Sophie-Rauschmeyer.

ANDY. But she's already upstairs. When she goes down in the morning it's going to say Reymshaur-Ephos-Ouvlie!

NORMAN. (*Goes* D. R.) Why do I bother talking to you?

ANDY. I'm going to meet Mrs. Mackininee. (*Crosses to door.*) If I'm still alive, I'll be back at two a.m. . . . If not, about three-thirty. (*He exits.*)

BLACKOUT

ACT I

SCENE 2

Lights come up.
Three days later. The room is empty. The door opens and Andy enters, carrying his briefcase, having just returned from another grueling afternoon of selling.

ANDY. . . . Hi, Norman, how's it going? (*He stops and looks at the desk, but Norman isn't there. He walks into room. He looks upset. He puts down briefcase* U. *of radiator and crosses to tape recorder.*) All right, Norman, where the hell are you? (*The telephone rings. Andy doesn't answer it. It rings again. He pushes the receiver into the waste paper basket. Then he picks it up.*) Hello? . . . Oh, Mr. Franklyn . . . I'm sorry I didn't answer the phone sooner, but I couldn't find it . . . I still have the bandages on my eyes . . . Oh, didn't I tell you? Well, the doctor says my only chance is to have the operation . . . The only trouble is, it's six hundred dollars . . . Yes, the same amount I owe you . . . But I'm determined to pay your bill rather than have the opera-

15

tion . . . Unless you have another suggestion . . . You like the first one best . . . (*We hear a pounding on the front door.*)

NORMAN'S VOICE. (*Off.*) Andy, hurry up. Open the door. I forgot my key. (*Andy crosses to door and opens it. Norman rushes in with a large package of groceries.*)

ANDY. Where've you been all day?

NORMAN. (*Taking groceries to c. table.*) In love. Don't talk to me now. I'm busy. (*Crosses to desk. Takes off jacket. Puts it on desk chair.*)

ANDY. I know you've been busy, but you haven't been working. I just looked on the desk; there are no new pages.

NORMAN. (*Goes upstairs to his room for a fancy basket.*) I've got plenty of time. Plenty of time.

ANDY. Not anymore we don't. We have three days. Three days to finish three articles.

NORMAN. I'm thinking all the time. I've got everything up here. (*He points to head and starts downstairs.*)

ANDY. One! Give me one article. Give me one title you've thought of since the day that Arkansas frangipani checked in here and you painted love letters up and down the staircase . . . Let's hear one title!

NORMAN. "The Real Case Against Fluoridation. Is Tooth Cancer Next?"

ANDY. Write it. Sit down and write it. Now!

NORMAN. Don't coerce me. I can't work under coercion.

ANDY. How about under savage beating? I got a life savings and three years of work tied up in this venture. And I'm not going to see something good and vital and worthwhile go down the drain because you can't think of anything else but that corn-fed Minnie Mouse next door. What's in that package?

NORMAN. Groceries.

ANDY. I buy the groceries. It's for her, isn't it? What have you got in there?

NORMAN. (*Indignantly picks up bag.*) None of your business. It's private groceries.

ANDY. (*Looks at package which Norman is holding.*) The United Nations Gourmet Shoppe?

NORMAN. They always have a big sale before Lent.

ANDY. (*Snaps his fingers and points to the table. Norman obeys and puts the bag down. Andy starts to take out some of the cans*

16

and jars and examines them.) . . . Miniature watermelon? . . . Baby Siberian herring filets? . . . Tiny kumquats? . . . Who's coming for dinner, a couple of midgets?

NORMAN. I had a yen for some delicacies. *(Goes L., below table, to the desk.)*

ANDY. Delicacies? You haven't eaten anything fancier than a banana and peanut butter sandwich since the day I met you. *(Puts the jars back. He reaches in bag and takes out the bill. He is shocked.) Twenty-two dollars??* You spent twenty-two dollars for toy food?

NORMAN. Take it out of my share of the profits.

ANDY. Your share of the profits can't pay for your banana and peanut butter sandwiches. Are you out of your mind?

NORMAN. I'm giving her a gift. You gave your mother a gift on Mother's Day, didn't you?

ANDY. I gave her a year's subscription to our magazine. You hardly even know this girl.

NORMAN. I know her. *(Goes to telescope. Andy crosses to desk for glue and dummy magazine.)* I know she works like a dog six days a week. I watch her through the telescope running after that bus every morning. I watch her coming home every night. Tired. Hungry. *(Goes L. to Andy.)* That sweet, beautiful girl coming home to nothing better for dinner than a can of Broadcast Corned Beef Hash.

ANDY. How do you know that?

NORMAN. I check her garbage every afternoon.

ANDY. All right, Norman, get a hold of yourself. *(Sits—pole table.)*

NORMAN. Get a hold of myself? Are you kidding? My functioning days are over. I've become an animal. I've developed senses no man has ever used before. I can smell the shampoo in her hair three city blocks away. I can have my radio turned up full blast and still hear her taking off her stockings! Don't you understand, SHE TURNS ME ON! From my head to my toes, I take one look at her and I light up. This month alone my personal electric bill will be over two hundred dollars . . . *(Starts putting jars and cans in basket.)*

ANDY. *(Glues a clipping onto page of dummy magazine.)* You know, when I first met you in high school, I thought you were eccentric. When we worked on the journal together in college, I

17

thought you were a very promising fruitcake. The last couple of years I decided you were a tremendously talented bedbug . . . Now I know what you are . . . (*Rises. A few steps* R.) *You are the unhatched egg of an illiterate looney bird!* We've got three days to get out a magazine and you spend your time buying pygmy cucumbers for a girl with strong shampoo?

NORMAN. I'm going to let that pass. I am also not going to waste time trying to explain something that cannot be explained. Because it would be a waste of time.

ANDY. You've already cornered the waste of time market. Explain it to me.

NORMAN. Did you ever hear of physical attraction? Pure, unadulterated physical attraction?

ANDY. I have.

NORMAN. What is it?

ANDY. It's when one hippopotamus likes another hippopotamus with no questions asked.

NORMAN. Exactly. Now it's five-thirty and my hippopotamus will be getting off her bus. Now leave me alone because I've got work to do. (*Takes cans and jars out of bag and puts them on table.*)

ANDY. All right . . . Look, I'll put the kumquats in the basket and you finish the article.

NORMAN. Who are you, Miles Standish? I'll put my own kumquats in the basket . . . (*Goes* L., U. *of Andy.*) A ribbon! I need a red ribbon. You got a red ribbon?

ANDY. Do I have a red ribbon?

NORMAN. Either you have a red ribbon or you don't. If you have a red ribbon, I'd like it for my basket, please.

ANDY. I'm not going to discuss red ribbons with you at this time.

NORMAN. In other words, you're not going to give me your red ribbon!

ANDY. That's right. Out of the *thousands* I have saved in my closet, I'm not going to give you a red ribbon.

NORMAN. (*Goes up stairs to landing.*) That's one I owe you, Andy. From now on I'm keeping score. (*He glances out the window.*) There's her bus. (*He looks through the telescope.*) I almost missed her bus account of you.

ANDY. Get away from that window.

NORMAN. Are you crazy? And miss Sophie getting off the bus? You know I wait for this all day. (*He looks through telescope, focusing it.*)

ANDY. (*Few steps* R.) Norman, write me two more articles and I'll buy you a bigger telescope. You'll be able to zoom right into her shoes. What do you say?

NORMAN. (*Looking through telescope.*) I could have missed her bus. Sophie is on that bus and I almost missed it.

ANDY. (*Crosses up the stairs to the window and puts his hand over the lens, covering it.*) Damn you, Norman, answer me!

NORMAN. (*Still looking through telescope. He screams.*) Oh, my God! Sophie! (*He looks up and sees that Andy has his hand covering opening.*) You idiot! I thought her bus fell into a hole. Get your hand off my lens opening!

ANDY. My hand stays on your opening until you make me a promise.

NORMAN. I promise! I promise! Now get out of the way. (*Andy comes down stairs.*) There she is! Oh, Mother in Heaven, will you look at that girl! Look at her! Just look at that girl!

ANDY. All right, let me see.

NORMAN. (*Screams.*) Stay away from here. (*Andy hangs up jacket on bulletin board hook, then sits on pole table.*) I'm looking at her. Oh, you wonderful crazy Sophie. She has got without a doubt the most magnificent ear lobes on the face of the earth. (*Looks out the window, straight down.*) She's in the building. She'll be upstairs any minute. (*He runs down the steps, picks up the basket from the table and goes to the desk.*) You're not going to give me your red ribbon, right?

ANDY. Who do you think I am, Fanny Farmer?

NORMAN. That's two I owe you. (*He sits at the typewriter, puts basket on floor and rips paper out of machine. Puts in another piece and begins to type.*)

ANDY. What are you doing? Are you working? . . . Norman, sweetheart, what are you writing? (*Rises and goes to peer over his shoulder. Reads aloud.*) . . . "Adomis terra amorta eternos" . . . What is that, a prescription?

NORMAN. It's "I worship the ground you walk on" in Latin. It goes with the groceries. (*He rises and puts note in basket. Faces Andy.*) Now get out of my way or you get Elberta peaches in brandy right between the eyes. (*Andy moves and Norman starts to the door as the telephone rings.*)

ANDY. (*Calls after Norman.*) Norman, you've got three minutes to deliver your Care package. (*Picks up the phone. Into phone.*) United Nations Gourmet Shoppe . . . Oh, hello, Mrs. Mackininee . . . How are you? . . . The beach this weekend? Gee, I don't know. I've developed this awful cough . . . Yes, I'm disappointed too.

NORMAN. (*Rushes in.*) She's got it! She's got the basket! (*Runs back to door.*)

ANDY. (*Into phone.*) Yes, I agree it would be a lot more fun than staying home and collecting rents. What time do you want to go?

NORMAN. (*Holding the door open and peeking through the crack.*) She's reading the note.

ANDY. (*Into phone.*) How?

NORMAN. She's moving her gorgeous lips and reading the note.

ANDY. (*Into phone.*) You mean I hold onto you and the surfboard at the same time? Won't that be a problem going through tunnels?

NORMAN. She's looking over here . . . Here she comes! (*Closes door and runs screaming to the* C. *table.*) Clean the apartment! Hurry up! (*He takes the grocery bag to* U. *of bar.*) Clean the apartment! (*Andy hangs up the phone.*) I'm shaking. (*Rushes* L. *to Andy.*) Look at that hand shaking. Andy, I'm scared to death.

ANDY. *You're* scared? I'm going surfing tomorrow with a daredevil landlady. They'll find me washed up in Hawaii. (*The doorbell rings.*)

NORMAN. Open the door! Open the door! (*The doorbell rings again. Andy turns to go.*) Where are you going?

ANDY. To open the door.

NORMAN. Don't open the door. I'm not ready yet. (*Norman putes his jacket around his shoulders and gets a pipe from the slanting desk, which he puts in his mouth—upside down. Then he sits above the desk and poses.*) Open it! Open it! (*Andy opens the door and Sophie enters carrying the basket. She seems quite upset.*)

SOPHIE. (*To Andy.*) Excuse me. (*To Norman.*) Mr. Cornell, ah have tried to be neighborly, ah have tried to be friendly and ah

20

have tried to be cordial . . . Ah don't know what it is that you're tryin' to be . . . That first night ah was appreciative that you carried mah trunk up the stairs . . . The fact that it slipped and fell five flights and smashed to pieces was not your fault . . . Ah didn't even mind that personal message you painted on the stairs. Ah thought it was crazy, but sorta sweet . . . However, things have now gone too far . . . (*Goes down to pole table.*) Ah cannot accept gifts from a man ah hardly know . . . (*Puts basket on pole table.*) . . . Especially canned goods . . . And ah read your little note. Ah can guess the gist of it even though I don't speak Italian. (*Andy sits on stool below kitchen bar.*) This has got to stop, Mr. Cornell . . . Ah can do very well without you leavin' little chocolate almond Hershey bars in mah mail box . . . They melted yesterday, and now ah got three gooey letters from home with nuts in 'em . . . And ah can do without you sneakin' into mah room after ah go to work and paintin' mah balcony without tellin' me about it. Ah stepped out there yesterday and mah slippers are still glued to the floor . . . And ah can do without you tying big bottles of Eau de Cologne to mah cat's tail. The poor thing kept swishin' it yesterday and nearly beat herself to death . . . And most of all, ah can certainly do without you watchin' me get on the bus every day through that high-powered telescope. You got me so nervous the other day ah got on the wrong bus. In short, Mr. Cornell, and I don't want to have to say this again, *leave me ay-lone!* (*She turns and starts to go.*)

NORMAN. Aside from that, is there any chance of your falling in love with me? (*Sophie turns.*)

SOPHIE. You are crackers, you know that, don't you? (*To Andy.*) Did you know your roommate is crackers? (*Andy crosses D. R.*)

ANDY. Yes, but I didn't know the exact medical term.

SOPHIE. (*To Norman.*) Didn't you listen to one solitary word ah said to yew?

NORMAN. Yes, I'm listening . . . (*Jacket off his shoulders as he rises and goes above pole table to Sophie.*) I'm listening, I'm looking and I'm smelling. (*Sniffs.*)

SOPHIE. (*Yells and backs R.*) Ah don't want to be smelled! (*Norman follows and sniffs again. She moves R. to Andy.*) Tell him to stop smelling me.

21

ANDY. (*Quietly.*) Norman, stop smelling her. (*Sits on sofa.*)

SOPHIE. (*To Norman.*) Ah am going to repeat this to you once more and for the last time. Ah am ingaged to be married to First Lieutenant Burt Fenneman of the United States Marine Corps. (*To Andy.*) And in six weeks ah will be *Mrs.* First Lieutenant Burt Fenneman of the United States Marine Corps . . . (*To Norman.*) an ah intend to be happily married to him for the rest of mah natural life. (*A step* L.) Do you understand that?

NORMAN. (*Goes* R. *to her.*) Please lower your voice. I'm trying to hear your hair growing.

SOPHIE. (*Goes* R. *to Andy.*) What is wrong with him? Does he have oral trouble?

ANDY. Oral trouble?

SOPHIE. (*Points to her ears.*) With his ears. Hard of hearing.

ANDY. Yes, he has very bad orals.

SOPHIE. Ah thought as much. (*Goes back to Norman.*) Ah could have yew arrested, you know that? For loiterin', breakin' 'n enterin', tamperin' with mah mail box, pesterin', peepin' tom'n! Don't think ah won't do it. (*Starts toward door.*)

NORMAN. (*Stops her.*) Then I'll have *you* arrested. For creamy smooth skin, perfect teeth, a ridiculously small nose, insanely gorgeous ear lobes and an indecently fantastic unbelievable fragrance. (*He inhales.*)

SOPHIE. (*Screams.*) Ah told yew to stop smelling me! (*To Andy.*) Do something!

ANDY. Do you want me to hold his nose?

NORMAN. (*Moves* R. *to her.*) I'm sorry. A girl who looks like you shouldn't be allowed to walk the streets. (*Grabs her* D. *arm.*) This is a citizen's arrest! (*Starts pulling her with him toward steps.*)

SOPHIE. (*Pulls away. To Andy.*) If he doesn't keep away from me, ah'm going to arrange to have mah fiance inflict bodily harm to him. Tell him that.

ANDY. Norman, her fiance is going to inflict your body with harm.

NORMAN. Do you think that would stop me? Beatings? Flailings? Whippings? I welcome them. Tell her!

ANDY. (*To Sophie.*) He says he welcomes beatings, flailings and whippings.

SOPHIE. Ah heard him!

22

ANDY. She heard you.

NORMAN. (On stairs.) If having a friend of yours punch me very hard is going to make you happy, my entire face is at your disposal.

SOPHIE. Hey . . . are we on one of those television programs or somethin'? If we are, ah'd like to know. Otherwise ah'm callin' Camp Pendleton.

ANDY. Don't look at me. I'm just an innocent bystander.

SOPHIE. So am I. Two years ago in Japan ah represented mah country in the Olympic swimming competition. In order to be a member of the Official Yewnited States Olympic swimming team, yew must be in one hundred per cent perfect physical condition. That's me. Ah was one hundred per cent physically perfect. *Until* ah moved next door. From the day ah found that trail of little heart shaped peanut brittles leading from mah door to his door, ah have been a nervous wreck . . . Not only is it difficult to keep up with mah swimming, but ah'm afraid to take a bath. Ah have found that when ah brush mah hair, mah hair falls out. And the ones that fall out have not been replaced by new ones . . . Ah am twenty-three years old and that man is starting me on the road to total baldness. Ah intend to get married while ah still have a full head of hair left. (*She goes to the door.*) Ah am now going to have a dinner of good, basic American food, clean mah apartment and get ten hours sleep. If ah see him sittin' in that big tree outside mah window again, strummin' that ukulele and singin' those Spanish love songs, ah'm gonna call for the United States Marines. (*She exits and slams the door. Norman and Andy stand there for a brief second in silence. Then a wild gleam of uncontrolled happiness flashes across Norman's face.*)

NORMAN. (*Goes to the kitchen.*) I'm getting to her, Andy . . . I tell you, I'm getting to her.

ANDY. The only thing you're going to get is bayonet practice . . . She's engaged, Norman, forget about her.

NORMAN. (*Coming out of kitchen.*) *Forget* about her? Did you see what was just in this room? Did you see?

ANDY. I saw. It was a girl.

NORMAN. (*Shocked. Comes down right to Andy.*) A *girl*? You call that a girl?? That's not a girl. *That* was one of God's creations made during his *best* period! Don't ever call her a girl in front of me again. (*He storms back into the kitchen.*)

23

ANDY. Well, whatever that thing is, if it goes bald, you're in big trouble with our armed forces.

NORMAN. (*Comes out of kitchen with a mop.*) I can handle Uncle Sam.

ANDY. Where are you going with that?

NORMAN. (*Crossing D. L. Empties wastebasket on floor.*) You think I'm going to let her clean her apartment after she's been working all day?

ANDY. (*Rises and goes to bar. Gets ukulele. Goes L. menacingly.*) All right, I've had just about as much of King Kong and Fay Wray as I can take . . . You move two steps away from that typewriter and for the rest of the week you'll be picking ukulele out of your head.

NORMAN. Not unless you're capable of swallowing an entire mop.

ANDY. Norman, what's happened to you? I've seen you panting over a girl before, but this is the first time I ever saw steam coming out of your ears . . . I'm worried about you.

NORMAN. Don't you think I am too? I am definitely worried about me. I was up all last night re-reading Krafft-Ebbing. In 1926 there was a case very similar to mine in Gutenburg, Germany. It involved a nun and a knockwurst salesman. (*He crosses to door with wastebasket and mop. Andy then goes L., leaves ukulele on U. L. table.*) But I can't help myself, because I'm crazy about that girl. I'll do anything, including mopping her kitchen floor, to be with her every night for the rest of my life.

ANDY. In six weeks she's marrying the Marine.

NORMAN. What she does during the day is her business. (*He exits. The telephone rings. Andy turns the tape recorder on to "Record" and talks into the mike.*)

ANDY. (*Chinese.*) On sing mah toh wan po soo chow moo ling. (*He turns machine off. The telephone rings again. He quickly reruns the tape. Then picks up the phone and speaks in Chinese dialect.*) Yes, please? Wo Pings Chinese Gardens. (*He turns the machine on and we hear his voice from before.*)

ANDY'S VOICE. Hey, Luigi, how about a little service? (*He quickly hangs up, turns off the machine. The door flies open and Sophie storms in angrily.*)

SOPHIE. (*Shouts.*) Do you know what he's doing? Do you know what he's doing now?

ANDY. He's mopping your kitchen floor.

SOPHIE. *He is mopping mah kitchen floor.*

ANDY. And you don't want your kitchen floor mopped.

SOPHIE. (*Screams.*) Ah don't want it mopped 'cause ah waxed it last night and now *he's moppin' up all the wax.*

ANDY. I can hear you. I have perfect orals.

SOPHIE. Don't you understand? He has illegally entered mah apartment and criminally mopped mah floor. Aren't you going to do anything except stand there?

ANDY. If you'll calm down, maybe we can discuss this?

SOPHIE. Of course. (*Crosses to desk.*) Ah just have to make one call. May ah use your phone?

ANDY. Certainly.

SOPHIE. (*Dials once.*) Thank you. Ah don't have one of mah own. (*Into phone.*) Hello? San Francisco Police. (*Andy closes door.*)

ANDY. You wouldn't.

SOPHIE. Wouldn't I? (*Into phone.*) Ah'd like to report a demented man who's run amuck in mah kitchen.

ANDY. (*Goes to Sophie.*) Will you just listen to me for two minutes?

SOPHIE. (*To Andy.*) In two minutes he will have mah wallpaper steamed off and sent out to be dry cleaned. (*Into phone.*) . . . That's right, run amuck . . . No, not with a knife, with a mop.

ANDY. (*He tries to restrain her by holding her shoulder.*) Give me sixty seconds.

SOPHIE. Take your hands off mah "engaged" shoulder.

ANDY. Give me that phone. (*He takes it from her.*)

SOPHIE. It's just gonna cost you another dime 'cause ah'm gonna call them again.

ANDY. Why won't you listen to me?

SOPHIE. Why? Ah'll tell you why. (*She crosses and picks up a lamp. She crosses back to him and turns the lamp on, holding it up to her cheek right in front of his face. Andy puts phone on desk.*) Look at mah skin. Those big, ugly red blotches are hives. Do you know what causes me to get hives?

ANDY. Holding a lamp to your face?

SOPHIE. Nervous tension causes me to get hives. And having mah floor mopped causes nervous tension. Ah am breaking out in

25

big red blotches and ah am losing mah hair and ah have a date (*Puts lamp back on desk.*) with mah fiance tomorrow night and ah'm going to look like a little old man with the measles . . . And you have the ultimate gall to ask me for time. (*Goes* R.—U. *of Andy.*)

ANDY. I know exactly what you're going through. I've lived with that nut for three years and he's turned my hair grey.

SOPHIE. (*Comes back* D.) Ah fail to notice it.

ANDY. (*Goes to Sophie.*) Look at my eyelashes. All grey. I used to have long, beautiful black eyelashes. Did you ever see anything like that before? Grey! Grey! Grey!

SOPHIE. (*Moves in close and gives them a close look.*) Grey eyelashes are not as noticeable on a man as a receding hair line is on a girl. (*Breaks* D.)

ANDY. (*Being solicitous.*) It's not receding. You have beautiful hair.

SOPHIE. Do you like it?

ANDY. Very much.

SOPHIE. I'm glad. Because a lot of it has fallen on your floor. And if he's not out of there in five seconds, a lot of his blood is going to be on mah floor . . . Ah'm gonna start counting before ah call again.

ANDY. No, you're not. You're going to sit down and listen to me. (*He gives her a gentle push towards a chair.*)

SOPHIE. (*Rises immediately.*) If you're threatening me ah'd advise you not to. You're tall and skinny and ah'm short and strong.

ANDY. Well, I'm glad you live next door. I have a lot of trouble opening jars . . . Can I tell you about Norman Cornell?

SOPHIE. Why not? Ah'm not doin' anything but countin' . . . One, two, three—

ANDY. He is impulsive, compulsive, irrepressible and incorrigible (*Sophie starts to interrupt, but Andy continues*) but he is also one of the most talented, creative and inspired young writers living in this country today. Will you accept that?

SOPHIE. Ah have never read anything of his except an Italian mash note in mah grocery basket . . . Four, five . . . (*Goes* L., D. *of Andy, to the desk.*) Ah'm usin' the phone.

ANDY. (*Rushes* L.) Not until you hear me out. (*Puts hand on phone.*) In his freshman year at Dartmouth he wrote a thesis on the economic growth of the Philippine Islands since 1930 without any previous knowledge of economics, the Philippines or 1930.

SOPHIE. There is no end to the talent of the mentally warped. (*Starts to pick up phone, but Andy's hand is there to stop her again.*) If ah have to scream, ah'll scream.

ANDY. He's been offered jobs to write for every news agency in the country, plus *Time, Look, Life, The Saturday Review* and *The Diners Club Monthly.* (*Guides Sophie into the chair above the desk. He goes U. L. of Sophie, and sits on desk.*) Please believe me when I tell you that Norman Cornell is not only one of the brightest young men in America today, but he is also the hope and promise of today's young generation and tomorrow's future. (*And in the door with mop comes the hope of tomorrow's future.*)

NORMAN. I just knocked your cat in the toilet. It was an accident. He's going to be all right. (*He rushes back out, closing door behind him.*)

SOPHIE. (*Rises and runs R., above table, to landing.*) Police! Somebody get the police!

ANDY. (*Running after her.*) All right, Miss Rauschmeyer, let's not panic.

SOPHIE. (*On steps leading to landing.*) That's easy for you to say. He's not out flushin' your cat into the San Francisco Bay. (*Comes down stairs.*) Gimme that phone.

ANDY. (*When he stops her, she starts kicking him.*) I promise the minute he comes back I'll thumb tack him to the wall. Stop kicking me. I have very thin socks.

SOPHIE. Either you let me call the police or ah'll smash everything in your house, startin' with the dishes. (*She runs into the kitchen. We hear a loud crash.*)

ANDY. Okay, if you want to play rough, then we'll play rough. (*We hear another crash. He charges into the kitchen after her. Now there is some yelling followed by dishes crashing, and pots and pans. Two seconds later he comes out, his arm twisted behind his back, followed by Sophie who is doing the twisting.*) All right, let go . . . I don't want to take advantage of you, so let go.

SOPHIE. Ah'm callin' the police and ah don't want any trouble from you.

ANDY. I won't give you any trouble if you don't give me any trouble.

SOPHIE. Are you goin ' to let me call the police?

ANDY. (*In pain.*) Yes . . . Yes . . . (*She lets him go. He rubs*

his arm and goes L. *around the pole table. Sophie goes to phone.*)
You ought to be ashamed of yourself, being stronger than a fellow.
SOPHIE. Physical fitness is as important as Godliness and Cleanliness.

ANDY. What about friendliness? And good neighborliness? Just hear me out and then if you're still upset we can go back to angriness and destructiveness. All right? (*She looks at him, then puts the phone back on the receiver.*) Thank you . . . Have you ever heard of a monthly magazine called *Fallout*?

SOPHIE. Is it anything like the *Reader's Digest*?

ANDY. It is nothing like the *Reader's Digest*. It is a protest magazine. And one of the things it protests against is the *Reader's Digest* . . . What *do* you read?

SOPHIE. Ah'm a religious follower of *Sports Illustrated*.

ANDY. Why did I ask? I'll try to explain what we do. (*Points to sign above bulletin board on* L. *wall.*) This is our credo, "A Remedy for a Sick Society" . . . (*Goes* L. *above pole table.*) We're not doctors, we're diagnosticians. We point to the trouble spots. I'm the editor and publisher. It's my job to get it printed and sold. Norman is our staff. He is fourteen of the best writers around today. Every word, from cover to cover, is his. Besides Norman Cornell, he is sometimes Abbott Kellerman, Professor O. O. Pentergast, Gaylord Heyerdahl, Jose Batista, Madame Pundit Panjab, Doctor Sydney Kornheiser, Major General Wylie Krutch and Akruma Oogwana . . . The kid is versatile . . . Now we may use assumed names, but we believe in what we write and in what we publish. (*Gets copy of* Fallout *from a pile of magazines under the* L. *end of desk.*) When you go back to your room, I would like you to read last month's issue, and then I want you to tell me if you think we've spent three years and every penny we have in the world for nothing. (*Goes* R., *with magazine,* D. *of Sophie, to below* C. *table.*) Tell me if the things we protest against every month in *Fallout* aren't the things you protest against every day in your everyday life. (*Sophie starts to interrupt.*) We have a modest business here, Miss Rauschmeyer. We don't make much money. If we sell every magazine we print each month, we make just enough to buy a new typewriter ribbon so we can get out the next month's issue. But we stay alive. And we love every minute of it. And we'll continue doing it as long as there is an angry breath in our body and as long as there is one single iota of corruption left in our society that's worth protesting about. (*Sophie makes a move to interrupt.*) But Miss Rauschmeyer, unless you smile at that talented lunatic in there and say "Thank you for your little Budapest sausages" . . . one of the great organs of free press will disappear from the American scene . . . (*There is a pause as he waits for her reaction.*)

SOPHIE. . . . Ah don't think we've been properly introduced.

ANDY. My name is Hobart, Andrew Hobart. (*Drops magazine on table.*)

SOPHIE. (*Goes* R. *to Andy.*) How do you do. I'm Sophie Rauschmeyer. (*Shakes hands.*) Mr. Hobart, ah appreciate the fact that you want to preserve the dignity of our nation. As ah told yew before, ah had the privilege of representing the United States in the Tokyo Olympics.

ANDY. I think that's wonderful! How did you do?

SOPHIE. Well . . . ah came in fifth. Not only was ah beaten by the U. S. S. R. and Poland, but ah also trailed behind Turkey and Egypt.

ANDY. I didn't know they swam in Egypt.

SOPHIE. Then you can imagine how ah felt representing the greatest nation on earth, coming in six seconds behind a little fat girl who was raised in the desert. (*Goes* L. *a few steps.*) Since the day ah disgraced them, ah have not been back to my home in Hunnicut.

ANDY. Hunnicut seems to disgrace quite easily.

SOPHIE. (*Comes back to the* C. *table.*) You don't know Hunnicut. In our schools we sing all four stanzas of the *Star-Spangled Banner.*

ANDY. I thought there were only three.

SOPHIE. Our principal wrote a new one. Since mah black day in Tokyo ah have made a new life for mahself. One that ah don't wish to jeopardize. (*Andy goes* U. *of* C. *table and goes to desk where he sits. Sophie follows him.*) Ah have found a nice job teachin' children to swim at the Y. W. C. A. . . . (*Andy starts licking envelopes and seals them.*) It doesn't pay much, but it keeps me wet . . . My parents, bless 'em, come up to see me twice a year from Hunnicut . . . (*He nods and licks envelope.*) But most important, ah have met, fallen in love with and intend to marry—First Lieutenant Burt Fenneman of the United States

Marines. (*She grabs an envelope from Andy, licks it and puts it down on the desk.*)

ANDY. I'm delighted you're going to marry a Marine. I hope you live happily ever after in the halls of Montezuma.

SOPHIE. Except he's not gonna marry me if he finds that wax moppin', cat drownin' lunatic in mah house.

ANDY. There's a very simple solution. (*Rises.*) I'll save your marriage and you'll save my magazine.

SOPHIE. How?

ANDY. (*Goes to* c. *table and picks up copy of* Fallout.) I promise to keep Norman away from you as much as possible. If when you see him in the hall or on the stairs you'll just smile at him. One hello from you will keep him happy for a long time. It'll keep us all happy. Will you do it?

SOPHIE. No!

ANDY. Will you do it for me?

SOPHIE. No!

ANDY. Will you do it for America?

SOPHIE. Well, if you put it that way.

ANDY. And will you please read this tonight?

SOPHIE. (*Goes* u.) All right, but you better keep him away from me.

ANDY. (*Follows.*) I promise you he'll never bother you again. (*Norman reappears with the mop.*)

NORMAN. (*Big smile.*) All finished. And the cat is fine. I gave her artificial respiration. (*He shows how with his two index fingers. Jakes the mop to the kitchen.*)

SOPHIE. (*Looks at Andy, then back to Norman as he comes back into the room and goes to tape recorder.*) Thank you.

NORMAN. (*Moved.*) Andy . . . she said "Thank you."

ANDY. I heard.

SOPHIE. Now if you'll excuse me . . . (*She starts for the door.*)

NORMAN. Norman. Say my name . . . Norman. (*Sophie looks at Andy.*)

ANDY. (*Shrugs.*) It's one little word. Norman.

SOPHIE. (*Reluctantly.*) Norman.

NORMAN. (*Holds the mike from the tape recorder.*) Would you say it in here? I'd like to have it to keep.

SOPHIE. (*Glares at Andy, who looks at her for a little under-*

30

standing. She sighs. Norman turns the machine on and she says into microphone.) Norman.

NORMAN. *(Turns machine off.)* Oh, that was wonderful. Thank you, Sophie.

SOPHIE. *(Turns and starts out. To Andy.)* Ah've kept mah promise. Live up to yours. *(She exits. The instant she's gone, Norman rushes over to the window and opens it, then rushes back to tape recorder.)*

ANDY. All right, Norman, I've just made that girl a promise. As long as you behave decently and normally and act like a sensible hum . . . What are you doing?

NORMAN. I want the world to hear it. From her own lips. *(Shouts out window.)* Norman loves Sophie and someday Sophie will love . . . *(He turns machine on.)*

SOPHIE'S VOICE. Norman!

ANDY. *(Afraid Sophie will hear.)* Turn that thing off!

NORMAN. *(Stops machine. Rewinds. Shouts out window again.)* Tell 'em again, Sophie! Who's the one who drives you out of your mind? *(He turns machine on.)*

SOPHIE'S VOICE. Norman! *(Sophie bursts into the room.)*

SOPHIE. *(Screams. Goes to pole table.)* Ah heard that. He is using mah voice in vain. That's against the law. Make him stop.

ANDY. *(Runs after her.)* He was just kidding around. He won't do it again.

NORMAN. I was just kidding around. I won't do it again.

SOPHIE. Stop embarrassin' me in front of mah neighbors. And that's the last time ah'm warnin' yew. *(Points her finger at him. Sees her fingernails.)* Look at that. Now mah nails are beginnin' to crack. *(She exits. Norman turns back to the tape recorder.)*

ANDY. *(Closes door.)* If you turn that machine on again, you'll be recording your own death.

NORMAN. I'll play it very low. She'll never hear me. *(To machine.)* Whisper it, Sophie. Tell me and nobody else. Who do you love? *(He turns machine on, lowering volume.)*

SOPHIE'S VOICE. *(Whispering.)* Norman! *(Norman falls to his knees as . . .)*

THE CURTAIN FALLS

31

ACT II

Scene 1

The next day. About 5 p.m.

The room is in pretty much the same condition, though the bills have been cleaned up from the floor around the desk and the dirty cup and coffee pot have been removed from the c. table. Two used coffee containers have replaced the stack of newspapers on the rattan stool. Andy's briefcase, the United Nations grocery bag and the bon voyage basket are no longer in sight. The tape recorder is missing from the desk as well as the clippings, but the dummy magazine is still there to be finished. A recent copy of Fallout is on the c. table. The ukulele is back on the kitchen bar. On the slant-top desk we now see two hair brushes and an electric cordless razor. On the sofa D. R. is an empty coffee can. Both doors are closed on the balcony.

There is no one on stage, but we can hear the slow, steady rhythm of a typewriter coming from Norman's bedroom. It stops occasionally, then proceeds to plod on. The front door opens and Andy enters carrying a small bag, his bathing suit wrapped in a towel, a terry cloth robe and in the other hand he carries a jar of Noxzema. He walks carefully and in pain, the result of an excruciating sunburn.

ANDY. Norman? (*The typewriter clicks away. Andy looks up at Norman's room and nods in relief. He throws the bag, towel and robe onto the sofa and puts the Noxzema in his jacket pocket.*) . . . I'm back! . . . I'm back from the beach . . . I have first degree burns on ninety-eight percent of my body . . . The other two percent is scorched . . . We went a half a mile out on the surfboard and there wasn't a God damned wave for three hours . . . (*The typewriter continues.*) . . . The only time I had shade was when a bird flew over me . . . You can see his

32

outline on my back . . . (*Starts up stairs.*) This is my eighth jar of Noxzema . . . (*The typewriter continues but no sound of Norman.*) . . . How's it going, Norm? (*Still no answer.*) Norman? . . . (*Now he's nervous. He starts up the stairs to Norman's room.*) Norman, you hear me? (*He goes into Norman's room. The typing stops. Andy returns carrying the tape recorder. He takes Noxzema out of pocket, unscrews the top and puts a dab under his shirt at the back of his neck. He winces as the cold meets the hot. He picks up the phone gingerly, then starts to dial but winces in pain after the second dial. With his left hand he takes some more Noxzema and applies it to the dialing digit of his right hand and then continues to dial. He then puts a little on his ear before applying the phone to that spot. Then he talks, in pain and softly.*) . . . Hello, Mrs. Mackininee? . . . It's me . . . Andy . . . I can't speak louder, my lips won't open all the way . . . No, the chattering stopped but now I have chills . . . I really don't think I'll be able to come down for that cocktail . . . Do you mind? . . . You *do* mind . . . Then I'll be down for that cocktail. (*He hangs up.*) . . . I sold my soul. (*The door opens and Norman steps in. He holds one hand over his eye which seems to be in some pain. Andy looks at him.*)

NORMAN. (*Calmly looking at Andy through his other eye.*) Why did you hit me with an apple?

ANDY. Why?

NORMAN. Yes, why? Why did you hit me with an apple? (*Goes to landing.*) What were you trying to do, take my eye out?

ANDY. I was trying to kill you but I'll take whatever I can get.

NORMAN. (*Going up to balcony.*) I don't think it's funny. Do you know what the impact force is of an apple falling three-and-a-half stories? . . . Forty-eight miles per hour. That apple was doing forty-eight miles an hour. (*Goes into room.*)

ANDY. You're lucky you didn't get a jar of Noxzema doing seventy-five! . . . I'm not going to ask you where you were, Norman, because I think I know where. I'm just curious as to why you came back. (*Norman comes out of his room, jacket off.*) Because there is nothing left for you here except physical mutilation.

NORMAN. (*Comes down the stairs.*) I came back because I have work to do. I believe we have a magazine to get out. (*Goes L. toward the desk.*)

33

ANDY. (*Goes* R.) Norman . . . don't play with me. I'm in a fragile state of mind.

NORMAN. If you'll excuse me— (*Norman puts handkerchief in pocket and sits. Puts a piece of paper in typewriter.*)

ANDY. Who are you kidding? What about the girl?

NORMAN. (*Looks straight at him.*) What girl?

ANDY. That star-spangled corn pone next door! I think I know where you were this morning, Norman. You were down at the delicatessen having a life-sized statue of her made in potato salad.

NORMAN. You're wrong, Andy. I'm no longer interested. It's over. Done. Finished. Finito.

ANDY. Is that a fact?

NORMAN. That's a fact.

ANDY. Then who did I hear in your room at three o'clock this morning playing "Prisoner of Love" on tissue paper and comb?

NORMAN. Me! That was me! But that was last night. And last night is not today.

ANDY. Something's happened, Norman, and I'm afraid to ask what. What's happened, Norman? (*Norman turns away from Andy. Andy goes* U. *to Norman's* L.) Look at me and tell me what happened!

NORMAN. (*Walking away*—R.) Nothing.

ANDY. You followed her this morning.

NORMAN. I don't want to talk about it.

ANDY. You waited for her outside the "Y."

NORMAN. (R. *of* C. *table.*) I did not wait for her outside the "Y."

ANDY. You went *inside* the "Y"?

NORMAN. (*Sits* R. *chair.*) I don't want to talk about it.

ANDY. You went inside and started yelling for Sophie.

NORMAN. I did not yell. I asked politely.

ANDY. *Then* you started to yell and they asked you to leave.

NORMAN. I don't want to talk about it.

ANDY. (*Goes* R. *to* C. *table.*) You didn't go all over the YWCA looking for her, did you?

NORMAN. No, I did not go all over the YWCA looking for her.

ANDY. Where *did* you look?

NORMAN. Just the swimming pool.

ANDY. (*Turns away.*) I don't want to talk about it.

NORMAN. They wear bathing suits, if that's what you're worried about.

ANDY. That's what I was worried about. What did she do, threaten to call the police?

NORMAN. She did *not* threaten to call the police.

ANDY. What *did* she do?

NORMAN. She *called* the police . . . They took me away in a patrol car.

ANDY. I knew it. I knew it.

NORMAN. (*Rises.*) You wanna hear my side?

ANDY. I'm not through with *their* side yet.

NORMAN. (*Sits.*) We live in a police state, Andy. Did you know we are living in a police state?

ANDY. (*Who can reason with this idiot.*) I know. First they start burning books. Then they keep the men out of the women's pools.

NORMAN. As we drove away I heard her screaming, "I hate you! . . . I hate you, I loathe you and I despise you. Hate, hate, hate, loathe, despise and hate!" . . . So I figured the best thing to do is forget about her.

ANDY. I think you made a wise decision, Norman.

NORMAN. I mean if she wants to play it cool, I don't have time to waste.

ANDY. (*He may be serious.*) Do you mean that, Norman?

NORMAN. (*Rises.*) I want to bury myself in work, Andy. Busy. I have to get busy again. (*Goes* L., D. *of table and Andy, to the desk.*) Just give me a typewriter and a lot of paper and then stand back, because you may get hurt. (*Sits at desk.*)

ANDY. I think you really mean it. That's wonderful! (*Goes to* U. L. *table, gets a pile of paper and hands it to Norman.*) Here. Type. No spaces, just lots of words.

NORMAN. What did I see in her, Andy? She's not bright, you know. Do you think she's bright?

ANDY. She has a native intelligence. Of a very remote country.

NORMAN. We have absolutely nothing in common. And how long does physical attraction last?

ANDY. An hour, an hour and a half the most.

NORMAN. Say it again!

ANDY. Sophie!

NORMAN. Say the last part.

ANDY. Rauschmeyer.

NORMAN. Now the whole thing.

ANDY. Sophie Rauschmeyer!

NORMAN. You're boring me. I've got work to do.

ANDY. (*Elated.*) Ah ha! I'll knock out the mailing list. (*Goes to* U. L. *table and gets clipboard with pencil attached. Goes to chair* R. *of* C. *table.*) You just sit there and write. If you want to eat or drink or smoke or go to the bathroom, you sit there and I'll do everything. (*Norman starts to type and he goes at it furiously. Andy sits and makes out the mailing list. Norman stops, looks at what he wrote, quickly tears it out of the typewriter, crumples it up, throws it away, puts another piece in and begins to type furiously. Then he stops, looks at what he wrote, tears it out of the machine, crumples it and throws it away, rises, paces* R., *sits and puts in another sheet of paper and begins to type. Andy looks up at this. The third time that Norman starts and stops typing is too much for Andy.*) Norman, if you're having trouble, maybe I can help you.

NORMAN. (*Looks up at him.*) What is today's date?

ANDY. Norman, the date isn't important. Just write the article. I'll fill the date in later.

NORMAN. (*Stares at the paper.*) You're right . . . Who cares about the date? . . . Boy, it's good to get back in harness again . . . (*He stares at the blank paper a moment.*) . . . And here we go . . . (*He adjusts the margin indicator.*) . . . You notice how I don't mention her name anymore?

ANDY. You're not concentrating, Norman.

NORMAN. You're right. You're right . . . You'd better get up on the roof because I'm opening the flood gates . . . Okay. We're all set . . . The paper is in . . . My fingers are poised . . . An idea is forming in my mind . . . Something is about to come out—

ANDY. Don't announce it, Norman! You're not a train conductor, you're a writer.

NORMAN. Maybe if I just started typing, something'll come out. (*He starts to type as Andy looks at him incredulously.*)

ANDY. I don't think that's going to work, Norman.

NORMAN. I can try, can't I? There's no harm in trying. (*He types. After doing a line, he stops and looks at it.*) Andy!

ANDY. (*Hopefully.*) Yes?

NORMAN. I think I'm going out of my mind.

ANDY. You're stale, sweetheart. You haven't written anything in nearly five days.

NORMAN. Did you see what I just put down on this paper? Zizzivivitzz! . . . Second in my class at Dartmouth and I wrote Zizzivivitzz . . . You wouldn't accept work like that from a monkey.

ANDY. Don't get hysterical on me, Norman.

NORMAN. (*Rips sheet out of typewriter and takes it to Andy.*) Here. Read it for yourself. What does that say?

ANDY. (*Resigned.*) Zizzivivitzz!

NORMAN. (*Crumples paper. Throws it on* C. *table and goes back to the desk.*) Don't tell me not to get hysterical. Maybe if I called her at the "Y" and tried to apologize . . .

ANDY. (*Rises and goes above table.*) She just had the police drag you away. Does it make sense for you to call her again?

NORMAN. You're talking to a man who just write Zizzivivizizz! . . . (*He picks up phone.*) I'll dial, you talk to her.

ANDY. Why should *I* talk to her?

NORMAN. Because my mouth dries up when I talk to her. No words come out, just little bla bla sounds. (*He demonstrates.*)

ANDY. If you did, Norman, you're going to bla bla to her yourself.

NORMAN. (*Glares at him, phone still in hand.*) You know what you are, Hobart? You're cold turkey. Cold turkey, lumpy stuffing and watery cranberry sauce. You have all the romance and sensitivity of a used car lot. (*He dials.*) You know what else you are? You're a sexual snob. You don't get really excited unless the girl has a straight-A average . . . Tell the truth, Andy, the sexiest woman who ever lived was Madame Curie, right?

ANDY. Right. I dream of her leaning over a low-cut microscope.

NORMAN. I don't need you. I'll talk to Sophie myself. (*Into phone.*) Hello? Is this the YWCA? . . . It is? Bla . . . bla . . . bla . . . bla . . . (*He quickly gives phone to Andy and goes* C.)

ANDY. (*Reluctantly talks into phone.*) . . . Miss Sophie Rauschmeyer, please . . . What? (*Norman hurries to Andy's side to listen.*) . . . When? . . . Why? . . . Where?

NORMAN (*Anxiously.*) What when why where what? What's happening?

ANDY. I see. Thank you. (*He hangs up.*) They just fired her!

37

They said it's the *third* time this week a mad man caused a commotion there. (*We hear a pounding on the door.*)

SOPHIE'S VOICE. Open this door or so help me, ah'll break it down.

NORMAN. Andy, help me. What'll I do?

ANDY. Get out of here. Let me talk to her. (*Doorbell buzzes furiously.*)

NORMAN. (*Starting upstairs.*) What will you say, Andy? What will you tell her?

ANDY. She's banging on the door. I can't audition for you now. (*Doorbell buzzes angrily.*)

NORMAN. (*Halfway upstairs.*) Just tell me one thing. Tell me one nice thing you're going to say about me.

ANDY. You never wear brown shoes with a blue suit. (*Doorbell again.*) Get out of here . . . (*Norman is climbing the ladder to the roof.*) Where are you going?

NORMAN. On the roof. If everything is all right, call me and I'll come down. If not, I'll jump down. (*He disappears through door at the top of ladder. The doorbell buzzes again. Andy goes to the door and opens it. Sophie enters—wet. Carries a YWCA duffle bag and a copy of* Fallout.*)

SOPHIE. (*Goes to foot of stairs.*) Where is he? Where is that insane, crazy, trespassin' lunatic? (*Andy closes the door.*) I know exactly what I'm going to do to him. I planned it all as I sat there drippin' all over the bus.

ANDY. (*Goes toward her.*) He's up on the roof, miserable and eating his heart out.

SOPHIE. Well, you can tell him not to bother. Ah'm gonna get a big dog to eat it out for him . . . Ah have been fired. They didn't even give me time to dry off.

ANDY. I know. I just spoke to the "Y." But it wasn't your fault. Didn't you explain that to them?

SOPHIE. Ah found it difficult getting their attention while a crazy man was chasing me all through the YWCA . . . And that present of his is still pecking away at everyone in the building.

ANDY. What present?

SOPHIE. The duck. He brought me a live duck. It's still there quackin' and snappin' at everyone. When ah left, the gym teacher was a-hanging from the basketball hoop and then that crazy bird chased a seventy-three year old Arts and Crafts teacher down to the swimmin' pool and off the high diving board.

ANDY. I didn't know about that.

SOPHIE. Well, did you know that ah've been locked out of mah apartment until ah pay mah rent which ah can't do because ah don't have a job.

ANDY. Look, we'll make it up to you somehow. I'll get you another job. Just give me a couple of days.

SOPHIE. (*Goes* L., D. *of Andy.*) Ah don't have a couple of days. Ah have rent to pay and food to buy. What am ah gonna do?

ANDY. There must be someone in San Francisco who needs somebody young and healthy and strong . . . I don't suppose you've ever considered professional football?

SOPHIE. (*Goes* D. *to phone on desk and starts to dial.*) Ah'm callin' my fiance!

ANDY. (*Goes toward Sophie.*) Wait . . . I have an idea. I don't say you're going to love it, but how would you like to come to work for us?

SOPHIE. Ah would rather get beaten in the Olympics by Red China.

ANDY. Why not? It'll pay your rent and buy you your iron and steel, or whatever it is you eat.

SOPHIE. (*Hangs up.*) Ah believe you're serious. If you're serious, ah suggest you make yourself available for our country's mental health program. Do you think I would work for that bomb aimed at the heart of America?

ANDY. What bomb?

SOPHIE. (*Few steps* R. *to Andy.*) Mr. Hobart, ah don't know if you're a communist, or a fascist, or just a plain old-fashioned traitor . . . But you are certainly no American.

ANDY. What are you calling me a traitor for?

SOPHIE. (*Picks up magazine from pole table.*) For this! For holding your country up to ridicule in black and white. All ah read last night was the table of contents, but if you don't like the country that gave you your birth, why don't you go back where you came from?

ANDY. I don't know what you're talking about, but writing constructive criticism about the degenerating American way of life is certainly not treason.

SOPHIE. I don't know what is in your government overthrowing

39

mind, but do you expect me to work for a magazine that publishes an article entitled . . . (*Goes* R., U. *of Andy, looks through pages.*) . . . "Is L.B.J. on L.S.D.?"

ANDY. We are not implying that he takes drugs. It's a symbolic alliteration meaning maybe the President in certain areas has gone too far.

SOPHIE. How about . . . "Twenty-Seven Ways to Burn a Wet Draft Card"? . . . Written from personal experience, Mr. Hobart?

ANDY. For your information, I happen to have served two years in the United States Army where I was interpreter for Brigadier General Walker Cooper.

SOPHIE. In what country?

ANDY. In *this* country. That idiot could hardly speak English! (*Tosses magazine on table.*) . . . My feelings about this country run just as deeply as yours, but if you'll turn down the national anthem for a few minutes, you'll be able to hear what some of the people are complaining about.

SOPHIE. Well, ah am one of the people and *yew* are one of the things ah'm complaining about.

ANDY. Well, fortunately, you're not in much of a position to complain about *anything!* . . . Look, if you don't work, you don't eat. If you don't eat, you get very skinny, you fall down and then you're dead. (*Goes* L., U. *of pole table.*) If you think your Marine will be happy living with a dead, skinny lady, that's his business. Personally, I think you ought to accept the meager bread I'm offering you.

SOPHIE. First you take away my loaf and then you offer me your meager bread.

ANDY. Why does everything you say sound like it came out of the Bible?

SOPHIE. Thank goodness yew heard of the book.

ANDY. Look, do you want the job or don't you? If you don't want it, *I'll* take it 'cause I need the money.

SOPHIE. Unfortunately, so do I. Just tell me why . . . why do yew want me around here?

ANDY. I'll tell you why. I *don't* want you around here. But that nut up on the hot tin roof wants you around here. You believe in your principles, I believe in mine. Mine is this magazine and I'll

40

do anything to keep it from going under water . . . that was an unfortunate choice of phrase.

SOPHIE. All right. That's your principle. Mah principle is breathing, eating and living, just like any other animal on this earth.

ANDY. So much for your character references Now about salary. What did you get at the "Y"?

SOPHIE. Seventy-two dollars.

ANDY. Norman and I both know how to swim; I'll give you fifty-five.

SOPHIE. For fifty-five dollars ah will come in early and poison your coffee. Ah want what ah got at the "Y." Seventy-two dollars.

ANDY. (*Reluctantly.*) So be it, you're hired. Your hours will be from ten to six, half a day on Saturday. Can you type?

SOPHIE. No.

ANDY. Can you take shorthand?

SOPHIE. No.

ANDY. Can you do filing?

SOPHIE. No.

ANDY. Maybe you'd better come in at eleven . . . Can you cook?

SOPHIE. Mah cat seems to think so.

ANDY. Okay, you can make lunches and pretend to look busy. Let's say you have two main functions. First, to keep out of my way at all times, and second, to *smile* at Norman as much as is humanly possible.

SOPHIE. Yes, sir. The first ah will do with the utmost dedication. And the second ah will do over mah dead body.

ANDY. (*Goes* R., D. *of Sophie.*) Miss Rauschmeyer, it's evident you and I haven't gotten along since you came to work here . . . We're both trying to make the best out of an impossible situation. You need money, I need you to say Goo-Goo to my partner once in a while. Now I suggest you roll up your lips and smile so we can get to work.

SOPHIE. All right, ah'll make mah bargain with the devil. Ah've never run from a fight. Ah'm ready to go to work. (*She extends her hand.*)

ANDY. Am I supposed to shake that?

SOPHIE. No, you're supposed to put seventy-two dollars in it.

ANDY. We pay at the end of the week. Company policy.

41

SOPHIE. Then ah'll start at the end of the week. Ah-don't-trust-you policy.

ANDY. All right, wait a minute. (*He crosses to side and gets milk bottles filled with pennies.*) There's seventy dollars in pennies. (*He gives her two bottles, takes third bottle and empties some of it in can on sofa.*) Minus Federal withholding tax and social security.

CURTAIN

(*While the curtain is down, we hear the sound of a typewriter over the house speakers.*)

ACT II

SCENE 2

A few days later.

Missing from the room now is Sophie's YWCA bag, all the crumpled paper from the floor, the coffee can seen on the sofa in the previous scene, the Noxzema jar and all of Andy's beach equipment. Half a dozen books are now occupying the shelf where the pennies were. The L. side of the C. table is set for lunch with a plate, knife, fork, spoon and napkin. A copy of Sports Illustrated *is also on the table.*

Norman is seated at the typewriter, his back to the front door. He is pounding away like a man obsessed. To his R., on the desk, is a pile of typed yellow pages. Despite this display of frenetic labor, Norman seems to be a happy man. Suddenly he stops as he seems stuck on something. He thinks a moment, then picks up a bell that is on top of his typed pages and rings it with a flourish. Sophie appears from the kitchen wearing a little apron over a bright orange dress and holding a dish towel. She looks at him.

NORMAN. Ubiquitous.

SOPHIE. (*Goes L. to the slanting desk where there is a large dic-*

tionary. She looks up the word.) Ubiquitous. U-b-i-q-u-i-t-o-u-s.
Ubiquitous. *(She closes the dictionary and marches back to the
kitchen.)*
NORMAN. Thank you.
SOPHIE. You're welcome. *(Smiles. Then exits. Once Sophie is
in the kitchen, Norman rises, goes to the slanting desk, gets the
dictionary and brings it to his desk. He puts it to his L. Sits at the
typewriter again and rings the bell. Sophie returns, tired. Carries bowl with mixing spoon.)*
NORMAN. Meretricious! *(Wordlessly, Sophie crosses L. to the
slanting desk, but discovers that the dictionary has been moved
to Norman's L. She quickly runs through the pages, stops and
reads from book, slowly and deliberately.)*
SOPHIE. Meretricious . . . M-e-r-e-t-r-i-c-i-o-u-s! . . . Meretricious! *(She puts the dictionary back on the desk, picks up her mixing bowl and starts to exit. Once past him, she turns and gives him
a huge, forced smile baring all her teeth. She continues to the
kitchen. He picks up the bell again and rings with a flourish. She
turns around.)* Stop ringin' that bell, ah'm not a cow!
NORMAN. Well, you don't like it when I call you Sophie.
SOPHIE. Ah'm an employee here, mah name is Miss Rauschmeyer . . . What is it, Mr. Cornell?
NORMAN. What's for lunch, Miss Rauschmeyer?
SOPHIE. Banana fritters, Mr. Cornell. Do you like them?
NORMAN. I love them. What are they?
SOPHIE. Fritters made with bananas. *(She starts to go back into
the kitchen, stops, turns and smiles. Then exits. Norman rushes to
the slant-top desk and quickly combs his hair, looking in the mirror on the wall above the desk. He quickly shaves with an electric cordless razor. Then he goes toward the kitchen.)*
NORMAN. . . . Do you notice the way I've calmed down? *(He
looks in.)* I'll never know how we got along without a secretary all
these—oh, let me help you with that. *(He goes into kitchen. We
hear Sophie shout and then a loud crash. Norman rushes out and
goes R.)*
SOPHIE. *(Following him, brandishing a pot.)* You try that with
your hands again and you'll have to learn to type with your nose.
NORMAN. Your apron was slipping. I was just tying it in the
back.
SOPHIE. And stop trying to get me into corners.

NORMAN. I'm not trying to get you into corners.

SOPHIE. Then how come this mornin' for ten minutes we had our heads stuck in the oven?

NORMAN. All right, don't be angry. Don't be mad at me. (*Goes back to the desk.*) You go back into the kitchen and I'll go back to work. See. See. I'm working again. (*He types.*) See. Working . . . (*She returns to the kitchen and after a moment of disgust, he resumes work. He is once more engrossed and does not hear or notice Andy as he comes in the front door. Andy looks exhausted from his outside activities. He looks over at Norman, whose back is to him typing away feverishly. Andy tiptoes behind him to get a better look at his work without disturbing him. He reads over Norman's shoulder a minute. He seems pleased with what he reads. To get a better look, he leans over and places his hands on Norman's shoulders. Norman closes his eyes upon feeling the hand on his shoulder. He turns his head and kisses Andy's hand.*) Forgive me! (*He notices that it is Andy's hand and jumps out of his chair and turns angrily to Andy.*) Are you crazy? You wanna give me a heart attack? Don't ever sneak up on me like that again.

ANDY. I didn't want to disturb you. You've really been working, heh? (*He picks up a stack of typewritten pages and begins to look them over.*)

NORMAN. I've been doing fine, fine.

ANDY. (*Looks around.*) Where's Esther Williams? (*Starts L., followed by Norman.*)

NORMAN. (*Follows.*) Shhh! I thought you were going to be gone all day.

ANDY. I couldn't take any more. (*Continues R., followed by Norman.*) I just flew under the Golden Gate Bridge with a crazy landlady pilot. Actually she did very well for a woman who just got her license yesterday. (*He continues to read Norman's pages.*)

NORMAN. Tell me all about it later. I want to finish this.

ANDY. She made three passes at the bridge. On the third one we had to pay a toll. (*Starts up stairs.*) Norman, this is good. It's better than good. It's brilliant.

NORMAN. I know . . . I know . . . (*Andy goes on up the stairs and into his room. Sophie comes out of kitchen carrying a frying pan with a banana fritter.*)

SOPHIE. Come on! Here's your lunch. Eat it while it's hot. (*Nor-*

man crosses and sits in chair L. of C. table. Tucks a napkin in his shirt.)

NORMAN. I like that. You're worried about me. (*Sophie tosses the fritter onto the plate already set on the table and returns to the kitchen. She re-enters, taking off her apron.*)

SOPHIE. (*Standing above the* C. *table.*) Would that be all now? If so, ah'd like to go home.

NORMAN. You could vacuum the rug.

SOPHIE. Where's the vacuum?

NORMAN. In that closet. (*Sophie leaves apron on the kitchen bar en route to the closet.*) I'll help you with it. It's very heavy. (*He goes into the closet after her and closes the door. We hear a loud crash. The closet door opens and Sophie comes storming out. She slams the door behind her. Norman does not appear. Andy rushes out of his room without jacket and comes running down the stairs.*)

SOPHIE. This time ah'm pressin' charges. (*She heads for the door.*)

ANDY. (*Carrying Norman's yellow pages.*) What's the matter? Where's Norman?

SOPHIE. You'll find him under the vacuum cleaner. (*She storms out and slams the door. Norman comes out of the closet, holding his head in pain and wearing the vacuum cleaner hose around his neck.*)

ANDY. (*To Norman.*) What did you do?

NORMAN. I bit her ear lobe! It was dangling right in front of my mouth. What did you want me to do, ignore it?

ANDY. (*Rushes to door and goes out in hall and shouts.*) Miss Rauschmeyer! Sophie! Wait a minute!

NORMAN. (*Follows Andy to the door.*) Tell her I'm sorry.

ANDY. Seventy-five dollars! I'll raise your salary to seventy-five dollars a week. (*Comes back into room—leaves door open.*) She's coming back.

NORMAN. (*Following Andy.*) Andy, you've got to square me with her just one more time.

ANDY. Norman, this has got to stop. She's becoming one of the highest priced secretaries in America . . . and she can't even type.

NORMAN. Tell her I've been working under a great strain lately. That I haven't been myself. Help me! What am I gonna do?

45

ANDY. (*Removes napkin and vacuum hose from Norman's neck and tosses them u. of kitchen bar.*) Go downstairs and buy a bottle of wine. We'll have a party just for the three of us.

NORMAN. (*Rushes to front door.*) That's a wonderful idea. I'll get a bottle of muscatel.

ANDY. Not muscatel. Champagne. Girls love champagne.

NORMAN. That's right. I'll take all my pennies and get a bottle of champagne. (*Starts R. toward the shelf where the pennies were.*)

ANDY. (*Grabs Norman, stops him and shoves him toward the door.*) No, you're right. Muscatel is better. Now get out of here. (*Norman gets to door just as Sophie returns. Norman hides his face with his hands.*)

NORMAN. Sophie, I just want to say. I know you hate me now, but bla bla bla bla bla . . . (*He runs down the corridor and disappears. Sophie ignores him.*)

SOPHIE. Where's mah three-dollar raise?

ANDY. You'll be drinking it in ten minutes.

SOPHIE. Ah knew ah shouldn't have trusted yew. (*She turns to go.*)

ANDY. I thought you never run from a fight.

SOPHIE. (*Turns back.*) Ah don't. Ah just had one in the closet. Mah ear is pierced now and ah don't even wear earrings.

ANDY. I told you it wouldn't be easy. I should have known you didn't have the guts to stick it out.

SOPHIE. Stick it out? Ah have been smiling at that idiot for three days. (*Gives big, forced smile as she comes back into the room to the c. table.*) You see that? That's what ah've been doing since ten o'clock this morning.

ANDY. Well, cut it out. You look like a demented ventriloquist. (*He picks up Norman's work and sits R. of table. Takes pencil from mug.*)

SOPHIE. Look, this was not mah stupid idea. It was your stupid idea.

ANDY. Well, it's a very smart stupid idea because it's working! (*He flourishes Norman's papers in the air as proof.*)

SOPHIE. It's working for you! You're getting your magazine. Ah'm gettin' holes in mah ears.

ANDY. I happen to be paying through the nose for those holes in your ears. It won't happen again . . . Now I've got fifty pages to edit so I'd like a little quiet, please.

SOPHIE. You won't even know ah'm here . . . 'cause ah won't be here! (*She starts for door.*)

ANDY. (*Turns and shouts.*) You'll be here because I'm paying you to be here and he's coming back in ten minutes and he *wants* you here.

SOPHIE. (*Closes door. Comes* D.) Then *here* ah will be! (*She sits* L. *of table angrily, grabs a magazine, crosses her legs and reads.*)

ANDY. (*Looks at her.*) This is not the Christian Science Reading Room. It's an office. And there's work to be done.

SOPHIE. Then do it. (*She continues reading.*)

ANDY. I'm talking about you.

SOPHIE. Would you like me to type a letter? Ah can have it finished a year from September.

ANDY. You can sharpen some pencils . . . and be quiet.

SOPHIE. Yes, Boss! (*Sophie glares at him, then gets up and goes to the radiator where there's a pencil sharpener. From a bowl, she takes one, inserts it in the sharpener and grinds. It makes a loud noise. Andy looks up, then goes over to her.*)

ANDY. What are you doing?

SOPHIE. What you told me to do.

ANDY. (*Pulls the pen from the sharpener.*) Thank you. I now have a ballpoint pen without a ballpoint. (*He goes to a tall vase on the kitchen bar and takes a feather duster from it. He goes back toward Sophie.*) Do you see this?

SOPHIE. Ah see it.

ANDY. First let me tell you that it is not a dead chicken on a stick. It's a feather duster. By that I don't mean you dust feathers with it. You hold it on this end—(*He demonstrates.*)—and you flick it against the furniture, thus dusting it. Do you think you could do that?

SOPHIE. . . . Lefty or righty?

ANDY. If you'd like, you can stick it in your pierced ear and shake your head. Just clean the room and be quiet. (*He puts the duster on the pole table, then goes back and sits in chair* R. *of table to continue working. Sophie glares at him, holding the duster.*)

SOPHIE. Yes, sir! (*She begins to dust the pole table, vigorously and angrily. Knocks magazines onto floor. Dusts U. L. table. She dusts her way across the room to Andy's chair L. of the C. table. Dusts under it—making some noise. Moves back to the C. table.)* Ah think ah'm gettin' the hang of it.

ANDY. Yes, you seem to be.

SOPHIE. *(Dusts bits of torn paper out of ashtray. Sings as she goes up to kitchen bar.)* "Yankee doodle went to town, riding on a pony, stuck a feather in his cap and called it macaroni" . . . *(Now is dusting the steps leading to the landing.)*

ANDY. You're not going to whistle the second chorus, are you?

SOPHIE. Ah just work here. Ah do what ah'm told. *(She starts to whistle. Andy gets up and crosses to her. He takes her wrist, leads her to the desk.)*

ANDY. All right. *(He takes some envelopes from the L. end of the desk and some stamps and places them before her.)* Here are fifty addressed envelopes and fifty stamps. You have a tongue. Don't talk. Lick. *(Takes duster from her and puts it on pole table. He goes back to chair R. of table and picks up the pages.)*

SOPHIE. *(Seated at the desk, holding the envelopes.)* Are these announcements for next week's cell meeting, Comrade?

ANDY. . . . No. Actually they're very thin bombs. You just add water. *(She laughs. Then she begins to lick the stamps one at a time and places them on the envelopes.)* I get the impression that you don't approve of me as a person.

SOPHIE. If that's what you are, that's what ah don't.

ANDY. Why not?

SOPHIE. Because ah don't approve of your character, your philosophy, your principles, your ideals, your vocation, your methods, your scruples, shall ah continue?

ANDY. Look, your opinions on anything have as much practical value as a 1939 calendar. I'm not paying seventy-five dollars a week to listen to a limited vocabulary. Be quiet and lick the stamps. I'm a busy man. *(He goes back to his pages.)*

SOPHIE. So was John Wilkes Booth the night he assassinated Lincoln.

ANDY. *(Stops.)* Are you implying I was in on the Lincoln job?

SOPHIE. Ah'm talking about your present activities. But ah wouldn't put it past you.

ANDY. Sorry, that night I was in Philadelphia cracking the Liberty Bell! *(He gathers his papers, rises and starts up the stairs.)*

48

I can't concentrate in front of the Senate Investigating Committee.

SOPHIE. The truth is always difficult to face . . . (*Stands up.*) Can mah tongue rest? The well has dried up.

ANDY. (*Stops on stairs.*) Look . . . if you're unhappy here, why don't you take a job as night watchman at the Statue of Liberty? Then you could swim around her at night checking to see if the torch went out.

SOPHIE. (*Going* u. *a few steps.*) "The enforcers of justice have always been the scapegoat of the enemies of freedom" . . . Do you know where ah read that?

ANDY. On the back of a Patrick Henry bubble gum card?

SOPHIE. (*Goes* L. *above pole table.*) No . . . in the speeches of Socrates. Did you ever read the speeches of Socrates?

ANDY. I'm waiting for the paperback to come out. (*He goes up to the balcony.*)

SOPHIE. (*Shouts up.*) It's out. That's where ah read it . . . It would shock you, Mr. Hobart, to know the amount of political literature ah have read.

ANDY. I would be nonplussed if you got into anything deeper than the names and addresses of the girls in the Miss America contest. I notice that your tongue is functioning again. Go back and lick the stamps. (*He goes into his room.*)

SOPHIE. And ah'm sure if it was left up to a *traitor* like you, no one would *win* the Miss America contest. (*She goes back to desk and stamp licking—standing up. Andy comes out of his room again, much angrier at the "Traitor" remark.*)

ANDY. You're right. I think a parade of pretty girls is fine. But listening to Miss North Dakota singing an aria from the "Barber of Seville" in the key of M, while baking an upside down seven layer cake in a hoop skirt she hooped herself, is beyond human endurance . . . I'll be very frank with you, Miss Rauschmeyer, up until now I'm not happy with your work. (*He goes back to his room.*)

SOPHIE. (*Glares after him. She is murmuring to herself and almost inaudibly says to herself:*) Ah suppose next he'll outlaw apple pie.

ANDY. (*Comes out of room.*) I heard that. I happen to love apple pie. Which, for your information, originated in Bavaria, Germany.

SOPHIE. (*Goes* L. *to above pole table.*) That's a lie. Apple pie is as American as blueberry pie.

ANDY. The only truly indigenous American foods are Thanksgiving turkey and chicken chow mein. (*He starts down stairs as she goes* R. *to meet him.*) You're deliberately distracting me from working on my magazine, aren't you?

SOPHIE. (*Returning* L. *to the desk. Back to stamps.*) Each citizen must do what he can.

ANDY. Of all the bigoted things— You haven't read one word in it past the table of contents.

SOPHIE. You don't have to drink the poison if it says so on the label.

ANDY. I'm going in the closet to work. Call me when Norman gets back. (*He goes* U. C.)

SOPHIE. (*Goes toward him.*) All right, tell me. Is there *anything* about this country you do like?

ANDY. I like almost everything about this country except people who like *absolutely everything* about this country.

SOPHIE. Why don't you answer mah question?

ANDY. Why don't you question my answer?

SOPHIE. Why don't you talk like a person so ah can understand which are the questions and which are the answers?

ANDY. Would it be all right if I worked in your apartment?

SOPHIE. It would not, if there's gonna be a fight, let's draw the battle lines on the field of the aggressor. And don't bother guessin' who said that 'cause ah made it up mahself.

ANDY. I had it narrowed down to you or Winston Churchill. (*Goes* R. *a few steps.*)

SOPHIE. (*Follows.*) *And* for your information, did you know Winston Churchill's mother was born in the United States . . . *in Brooklyn!*

ANDY. You'd never know it from the way he talked. (*Goes to door,* D. *of Sophie.*) Why don't you go back to your apartment and make some chitlins or grits? Your cat must be hungry. (*He opens door for her.*)

SOPHIE. (*Sits* R. *of* C. *table.*) Ah'm not leavin' until you admit you are snide, smug and narrow minded.

ANDY. Will you settle for belligerent?

SOPHIE. Ah will accept deceitful and treacherous.

ANDY. (*Slams door. Comes* D. *to bottom step.*) Okay, I'm deceitful and treacherous. And *you* are provincial and old-fashioned, antiquated, unrealistic, unimaginative, unenlightened, uninformed, and unbelievably unable to understand anything that isn't under water . . . (*Sophie rises.*) Your big trouble in life is that you were born a hundred and fifty years too late. You should have been at Bunker Hill loading muskets, raising flags and waiting for the British to show up with the whites of their eyes. Well, you may be shocked to learn that this is 1966 and this country has a whole new set of problems. But you wouldn't know about that because I don't think you're a real person of flesh and blood with feelings and sensitivities. I don't think you could be capable of having a genuine emotional attachment for another human being unless it was first passed by Congress and amended to the Constitution and painted red, white and blue. (*Goes to L. of pole table.*) If you've been listening carefully, Miss Rauschmeyer, I have just made a point.

SOPHIE. (*Goes to door, opens it, then slams it shut.*) All right, if you wanna make points, then ah'm gonna make one. Ah'm gonna make the biggest point you ever heard.

ANDY. (*Goes to sofa. Tosses pages on sofa.*) When you get to it, raise your right hand. With you it's hard to tell.

SOPHIE. You'll *know* when ah'm makin' it only you're not gonna like it. Are you listenin'?

ANDY. With one ear. That's all I need with you.

SOPHIE. Then here goes. (*Comes D. to Andy.*) Ah don't like you for a lot of the reasons ah already said. But the main reason ah don't like you is because ah am engaged to Lieutenant Burt Fenneman of the United States Marines. And in a few weeks we're supposed to get married. But for some insane reason that only a Hungarian psychoanalyst could explain, ah have suddenly discovered, and here comes the part ah was telling you about, that *ah am physically-attracted-to-you!* . . . Now, how do you like *that* for a point? (*And she storms out slamming the door behind her. Andy does not react. He just stands there. Suddenly the door flings open again and Sophie stands there glaring at him, hands on her hips.*) Did you hear what ah said?

ANDY. (*Without emotion.*) I heard. I heard what you said.

SOPHIE. (*Slams door.*) Well, how do you like them apples?

ANDY. *Those* apples.

51

SOPHIE. (*Goes to above* c. *table.*) *Them* apples. How do you like them?

ANDY. Are you serious?

SOPHIE. (*Yelling.*) Of course ah'm serious. There is something about your physical presence that appeals to me—and ah am as repulsed by it as you are.

ANDY. You couldn't possibly be.

SOPHIE. There is no earthly reason why ah should like *anything* about you. And ah don't. But ah do! What do we do about it?

ANDY. If you're looking for another boost in salary, this is not the way to get it. (*He starts up stairs.*)

SOPHIE. Where are you goin'?

ANDY. To get Norman's copy of Krafft-Ebbing. You're a bigger nut than he is.

SOPHIE. You don't believe me.

ANDY. I *believe* you. I just don't *understand* you. (*Comes back down steps.*) What do you mean you're physically attracted to me?

SOPHIE. Do you want a complete rundown of arms, legs, hair and teeth? Go get a pencil and paper and we'll take it item for item.

ANDY. You mean you like the way I look?

SOPHIE. Not terribly.

ANDY. You like the way I walk?

SOPHIE. Not really.

ANDY. You like the way I dress?

SOPHIE. Not remotely.

ANDY. Then what *do you like*?

SOPHIE. *Ah like the way you smell!!* (*Andy turns and looks to heaven or anyone else for some help.*)

ANDY. Oh, Sophie, Sophie, Sophie!

SOPHIE. And don't call me Sophie Sophie Sophie. Ah'm attracted to you but I still don't like you.

ANDY. That's impossible.

SOPHIE. Ah know. You are the most irritating, nauseating man ah have ever met in mah life—and if you tried to kiss me right now ah would not stop you. You wanna work on that for a while?

ANDY. (*Turns in despair. Goes to landing.*) No, I think I need outside help.

SOPHIE. Ah suppose you wanna know what started it all?

ANDY. (*Turns to a wall and just faces it.*) No, I don't.

SOPHIE. Yes, you do.

ANDY. Yes, I do. What started it all?

SOPHIE. It was your grey eyelashes. Ah have never met a man in your age bracket with grey eyelashes. I think it's *dumb* to have grey eyelashes, but ah'm very glad you have them . . . Now can ah ask you a question?

ANDY. Yes, you may ask me a question.

SOPHIE. Do you have any desire whatsoever to touch me?

ANDY. What does that mean?

SOPHIE. Which is the part you don't understand, desire or touching?

ANDY. (*Goes D.*) I understand both parts, I just never thought about it.

SOPHIE. (*Follows.*) Well, *think* about it . . . Time's up! Do you want to touch me or don't you?

ANDY. You've been spiking your fritters with bourbon, haven't you?

SOPHIE. Ah am being honest with mah emotions because that's the only way ah know how to deal with them. (*She moves closer to Andy.*) The plain disgustin' truth is ah would like to stand very close to you and feel your breath somewhere on mah neck.

ANDY. You shouldn't tell me that.

SOPHIE. Ah know it but it just comes out. Is there any possibility of you havin' the same disgustin' feeling about me?

ANDY. If I did it wouldn't be disgusting and if I found it disgusting I wouldn't have the feeling.

SOPHIE. Ah don't think ah got that but touché anyway.

ANDY. (*Moves into R. corner.*) And will you stop following me around the room?

SOPHIE. Ah'm not followin' you. You're runnin' from *me!*

ANDY. I'm running because you're following. Stay over there!

SOPHIE. Ah can't *smell* you from over here!

ANDY. (*Exasperated.*) What am I going to do with you?

SOPHIE. Ah gave you a suggestion, you didn't do it.

ANDY. Listen, you, for an All-American girl with a complete set of eagle scout principles, how do you explain being engaged to one man and attracted to another man?

SOPHIE. Very simple explanation. Ah can't explain it.

ANDY. What about your fiance?

SOPHIE. He can't explain it either.

ANDY. You mean you *told* him?

SOPHIE. Certainly ah told him. We're engaged.

ANDY. Oh, God, I'm afraid to ask what his reaction was.

SOPHIE. You may well fear. He wants to kill you.

ANDY. WHY? WHAT DID I DO?

SOPHIE. What did ah do when that lunatic friend of yours chased me all over the YWCA? It's nobody's fault. It's something that just happened.

ANDY. (*Escapes from her by going* L., *below Sophie, between* R. *chair and* C. *table to* L. *of table.*) Well, make it unhappen. If I'm going to get killed by a man in uniform, let it be the enemy.

SOPHIE. Ah am tryin' just as hard as ah can to make it unhappen. The minute you do anything physically repulsive, we'll all be a lot better off. (*Andy looks at her and then in an effort to be physically repulsive he knocks over the director's chair and goes to her, grabs her and gives her a hard, vicious kiss. Then he pushes her back and returns* L. *Looks at her.*) Ah liked it. We're in big trouble.

ANDY. What do you mean, *we're* in big trouble? *I'm* the one who's in big trouble.

SOPHIE. Are you going to yell at me or are you going to do something about our predicament?

ANDY. I'M GOING TO YELL AT YOU! YOU'RE GOING TO RUIN EVERYTHING I EVER WORKED FOR IN MY ENTIRE LIFE! WHY DON'T YOU GO BACK INTO THE OCEAN WITH THE REST OF THE FISH? (*She smiles.*) WHAT ARE YOU SMILING AT?

SOPHIE. Ah like it when you yell at me?

ANDY. . . . I don't care what you like. WHAT ARE WE GOING TO DO????

SOPHIE. How should ah know? But until we think of somethin', why don't you kiss me again? (*Andy charges at her with a threatening finger.*)

ANDY. You are without a doubt—the most—you—ah—oh, the hell with it. (*He goes* R., *takes her in his arms and kisses her. He's not quite sure why, but at this point common sense is beyond all reasoning. Sophie puts her arms around his neck and solidifies the kiss. The door flies open and Norman springs in happily, a bottle of muscatel in a brown paper bag in his hand.*)

54

NORMAN. (*Singing.*) "She loves me, but . . ." (*He stops and freezes as he catches them in the embrace. He looks at Andy and Sophie.*) . . . The least you could have done was chipped in for the wine!

THE CURTAIN FALLS

ACT III

The next day. Early afternoon.
There is one open suitcase, D. of the kitchen bar. A duf-
fle bag is on the sofa next to the portable typewriter
. . . all ready to go. The luncheon dishes have been
cleared and the feather duster returned to the kitchen
bar. The stamped envelopes and the manuscript pages are
no longer on the desk, but the dummy magazine is still
there, unfinished. The telephone is back on the pole table
along with a large pile of magazines near the pole. U.,
unseen by the audience, is an eight-pack of empty coke
bottles. Andy's clip-board is on the C. table.
Norman appears from his room at the top of the stairs
carrying a pile of books. He leans over the railing and
drops the books like a load of bombs into the open suit-
case below.
The front door opens and Andy enters, a very morose
looking young man. He looks up at Norman who tosses
his head. Norman is trying to convey all his anger and
bitterness in this one gesture.
The telephone rings. Andy closes the door, crosses to the
pole table and answers the phone.

ANDY. (*Into phone.*) . . . Steingarten's Beergarten . . . Oh
. . . Mrs. Mackininee . . . No, I'm not trying to avoid you. I
have a little answering service on the side . . . Yes, I called you
earlier because I was wondering if I could beg off tonight's Karate
party . . . Well, I'm sure the Takoshimos are a lot of fun, but
I'm awfully tired . . . I just don't think I'm up to an entire
evening of being thrown against the wall . . . (*Norman comes
out of his room carrying an enormous five-foot square blowup
photograph of Albert Einstein.*)
NORMAN. (*Not to Andy directly.*) Railway Express will pick it
up in the morning. (*He leans picture face to the wall and goes
back into his room.*)

ANDY. (*Back into phone.*) . . . Mrs. Mackininee, I definitely don't think I can make it tonight. I have some urgent business here . . . No, I'm positive I can't . . . Mrs. Mackininee, I think this is hardly the time to discuss a rent increase . . . Well, for that matter, I couldn't even pay a fifteen percent *decrease!* . . . All right, if that's how you feel about it, you can pick up your apartment in the morning. (*He hangs up. Norman comes out of his bedroom carrying a flower box with a few tiny leaves starting to sprout. He carries it down the stairs.*)

NORMAN. I'm taking the marijuana plant. (*He puts the plant on the kitchen bar. He starts for the stairs again.*)

ANDY. . . . Is this your final decision?

NORMAN. (*Crosses to tape recorder, turns it on, picks up speaker and switches on to record.*) It's my final decision. This is a recording. (*He switches it off and starts* U. R.)

ANDY. Because I think you're making a mistake.

NORMAN. (*Stops at bottom of stairs.*) I've only made two mistakes in my life. One was trusting you as my friend . . . and the other was going out for the muscatel. (*He continues up the stairs.*)

ANDY. Norman, I've known you for eight years. Can you ever remember me lying to you *once* in all those eight years?

NORMAN. Yes. I've known you for nine years. (*He continues up stairs.*)

ANDY. All right, *nine* years. I don't care what you saw yesterday, I'm telling you the truth. I cannot abide that girl and she finds me snide, smug and repulsive.

NORMAN. (*Stops.*) I see. And I walked in just as she was sinking her fangs into your throat, and you fought off the attack with your mouth.

ANDY. (*Goes* U. C.) No, she was kissing me.

NORMAN. Kissing *you?* . . . You're a foot taller than she is and you can't stand her. So the way I see it, the only way she could have kissed you against your wishes is for her to have nineteen inch lips . . . and I just don't buy that.

ANDY. I don't care what you're buying, I did not make an overt act towards her.

NORMAN. (*Comes out of his room.*) In other words, she was the one who did the overting.

ANDY. Correct.

57

NORMAN. Why?

ANDY. Well—that's beside the point.

NORMAN. I think not. Why did she overt you right on the mouth?

ANDY. You're gonna laugh.

NORMAN. Try me.

ANDY. . . . She likes the way I smell.

NORMAN. (*Looks at his watch.*) It is now three o'clock. I will be hysterical until three-fifteen. (*Goes back into room.*)

ANDY. What's so insane about it? *You* like the way *she* smells.

NORMAN. (*Storms out.*) How can you even *mention* the two smells in the same breath? (*Exits to his room.*)

ANDY. Norman . . . (*Takes off raincoat and tosses it on a high stool* U. L. *between the table and stairs.*) You mean to tell me that after nine years of a personal, meaningful relationship, you would let that flag waving sea urchin come between us?

NORMAN. (*Comes out of his room and goes down stairs to landing.*) I can live with a slob, a sadist, a forger or a junkie. I draw the line at finks. (*Goes to the light fixture on landing and removes one bulb.*)

ANDY. (*Breaks* D. *to desk.*) And what about the magazine?

NORMAN. (*Comes down stairs to suitcase.*) The magazine is no longer my concern. (*Puts bulb in suitcase. Goes above kitchen bar for an eight-pack of empty coke bottles. Takes half the bottles and packs them in the suitcase.*)

ANDY. You—hypocrite! You pretend to be devoted and dedicated to an ideal that we've literally starved for, and you can blithely toss it all aside because we're suddenly embroiled in a romantic triangle.

NORMAN. (*He goes to Andy.*) *Now* I know why this magazine never made a cent. *Now* I know why we were starving. You, me, the girl and the Marine is a quadrangle, not a triangle! You can't add! (*Goes* R. *to suitcase.*)

ANDY. And what do you think you're going to do once you leave here?

NORMAN. In exactly thirty minutes I have an interview for a job with the A.P.

ANDY. Working at the checkout counter?

NORMAN. Not the A *and* P, you idiot. The A.P.! The Associated Press.

ANDY. Doing what?

NORMAN. I'm a writer. They'll pay me for writing . . . Just as, I imagine, you'll make your living by *finking!* (*Goes to closet.*)

ANDY. (*Goes* L. *to* U. *of pole table.*) A writer? Without me to push you, prod you and encourage you, you couldn't hold down a job writing Rhode Island license plates.

NORMAN. (*Comes out of closet carrying two jackets on wooden hangers. Goes* L. *to Andy.*) No? . . . LJ Seven one nine six! . . . And there's plenty more ideas where that came from. (*Gives the jackets to Andy and takes the coat hangers to the duffle bag.*)

ANDY. All right, so we don't get along. Gilbert and Sullivan didn't speak to each other for fourteen years and they wrote twenty-three operettas together. Why can't we?

NORMAN. (*At* R. *sofa.*) Gilbert never walked in and caught Sullivan kissing Poor Little Buttercup.

ANDY. (*Puts jackets on* U. L. *table. Then goes* R. *to short wooden stool.*) Okay, Norman, if I have to fight for my magazine, I'll fight for it.

NORMAN. (*Looks at him in disbelief.*) You're joking, surely.

ANDY. Surely not.

NORMAN. Andy, I'm warning you. I'm not wiry, but I'm thin. I'll cut you to ribbons.

ANDY. I've already faced death with our paratrooper landlady. I'm not afraid of a skinny typist. (*Takes short stool* L. *of entrance stairs, to the door. He sits on it and crosses legs in Gandhi fashion.*)

NORMAN. (*Looks at him.*) What is that supposed to be?

ANDY. What does it look like? It's a *sit-in!*

NORMAN. (*He looks around to see if any sane person heard this lunatic remark. Then he moves up to the door.*) If you don't get up from that sit-in, you're gonna see a *punch-down!*

ANDY. Is that your answer to passive resistance?

NORMAN. No, my answer to passive resistance is active kicking . . . Get up! What do you think you're doing?

ANDY. The same as they did in Bombay in 1947 when twelve thousand Indians threw themselves across fifteen miles of railroad tracks.

NORMAN. (*Looks at his watch—goes to suitcase, closes it and picks it up. Goes to Andy.*) Well, Charley, in thirty seconds the five-fifteen is coming through.

ANDY. (*Steeling himself.*) Thou shalt not pass!

NORMAN. Thou shalt bleed from both ears!

ANDY. You would hit a man who wouldn't raise his arms in defense?

NORMAN. Actually I prefer it that way.

ANDY. Norman, if you go over to their side it's the end of free, creative thinking. They'll have you writing weather reports and shipping news.

NORMAN. In two minutes I bring in my first story about a dead man leaning against a door.

ANDY. (*Looks at him, then gets up.*) All right, Norman . . . (*Returns stool to R. of radiator.*) I had hoped to avoid bloodshed . . . (*Takes off sweater.*) But you leave me no recourse. The pain I am about to inflict is done purely on request.

NORMAN. (*Looks at him in disbelief.*) Do you mean it is your intention to actually come to blows? Hard hitting and everything?

ANDY. (*At pole table, rolling up shirt sleeves.*) My fist right on your deviated septum.

NORMAN. Knowing full well that on July sixteenth I finish a three-year course in Oriental combat?

ANDY. I intend to compensate by fighting dirty.

NORMAN. (*Puts down his suitcase, takes off his jacket and puts it on the landing.*) Okay, Andy, as long as you know the score. I've been waiting six months to try this in a real-life situation. I had hoped my first victim would be a mugger, but you'll do nicely. (*Goes to C. table, as he rolls up shirt sleeves.*) Oh, by the way. It's my legal obligation to warn you that Karate may be hazardous to one's health.

ANDY. And let me warn you that I have never once in my life struck another human being in anger. (*Both Andy and Norman pick up the C. coffee table and carry it R.*) I don't want to kill you, but I have no idea how strong I am. (*Goes L. and takes director's chair to R. of desk.*) If you feel yourself dying, just speak up. (*Norman tries to lift the R. chair with one hand. Andy comes to his rescue. Norman then carries the chair U. R. and puts it down near the table. Bows to chair.*)

NORMAN. Anytime you're ready.

ANDY. I'm ready if you are. (*Norman assumes a sort of professional pose while Andy just tries to look menacing.*)

60

NORMAN. (*Smirks.*) Is that the way you're going to stand? You don't know the first thing you're doing. You won't last ten seconds.

ANDY. When you're able to talk again, you can teach me.

NORMAN. . . . Can I show you the four basic positions? I'm still going to break your neck, but at least you'll look better. (*He goes toward Andy, who growls at him.*) This is ridiculous. You have no defense at all. I'm not even enjoying this. (*Goes* R.)

ANDY. If you want entertainment, turn on the television. If you want to fight, come over here.

NORMAN. I want to fight . . . (*In true Karate fashion, Norman takes a step towards Andy and swipes at the air twice and grunts audibly in Japanese fashion. He repeats the move with the other hand and the sound.*)

ANDY. If you're gonna do that, why don't you put on those big white bloomers like the Japanese wear?

NORMAN. You must be out of your mind. (*Holds up his poised right hand.*) Don't you realize this is a lethal weapon? This hand is trained to kill. Once I start it in motion, it can't be stopped. It's been trained that way. All right, Andy, I'm through toying with you. I'm gonna give you one chop . . . (*Looks at his watch.*) and then I've got to go. (*Norman approaches Andy. He raises his hand. Andy runs* U. *of the pole table and goes* R. *Norman follows him.*) Damnit, Andy, why don't you stand still and fight like a man?

ANDY. Because I'm afraid, that's why.

NORMAN. I told you that before we started.

ANDY. Not of you, of myself. I am so seething, so fed up with your monumental stupidity and infantile behavior, that if I get within two inches of you, I swear by everything I believe in this world, I'll crack your head wide open.

NORMAN. Then you'd better do it to me before I do it to you.

ANDY. All right, damnit, here!! (*And in a Karate-type swipe, Andy swings at Norman, who simultaneously swings at him with an identical blow, but they succeed in landing both blows on each other's arms between the wrist and elbow, causing enormous pain to both. They both stop and rub their painful arms and moan together.*) . . . Oohhhh . . . Oh, boy, that hurts . . .

NORMAN. (*Grimaces.*) Oh, God, my arm, my arm.

ANDY. (*Goes toward him.*) Are you all right?

61

NORMAN. (*Goes away to pole table.*) Let me alone. Why don't you look where you're hitting? In Karate you hit the neck or the kidneys, not the arm. (*Looks at his wrist.*) Ah, damn.

ANDY. What's wrong?

NORMAN. You broke my Benrus watch.

ANDY. (*Few steps* L.) Let me see.

NORMAN. It's broken. It's broken. There's nothing to see . . . it's my good watch, too.

ANDY. I'm sorry.

NORMAN. And I just put in a new crystal . . . and I had it cleaned.

ANDY. Why didn't you take the watch off first?

NORMAN. Because I didn't expect to get hit on the wrist. I told you you didn't know what you were doing . . . I don't want to fight anymore. (*Goes* R., D. *of Andy.*)

ANDY. Well, what are we gonna do?

NORMAN. (*Putting on his jacket.*) You can do whatever you want, I'm going.

ANDY. For good?

NORMAN. For good. I really don't like you anymore.

ANDY. (*Turns away.*) Okay, Norman, if you wanna go, then go. I think you're wrong, but if that's what you want, (*Goes* L. *to desk.*) I wish you the very best of luck.

NORMAN. (*Looking at his watch again.*) Boy, I really loved this watch, too.

ANDY. (*Goes* U. *of pole table. Norman goes to suitcase.*) So, this is the end of *Fallout* magazine . . . you've got to admit it, Norm, for a while we had a good thing going here.

NORMAN. (*Points to watch.*) If I knew what time it was, I'd hang around another ten minutes and watch you cry.

ANDY. You don't think I'm sincere about our friendship.

NORMAN. (*Picks up suitcase.*) For this magazine you would sell your own mother—who, incidentally, no one has seen for three years.

ANDY. Norman, please believe me when I say I'd rather have a handshake from you right now—than the Pulitzer Prize. (*He extends his hand out to Norman. Norman looks at him, puts down his suitcase and goes* L. *to Andy who stands* L. *of the pipe.*) . . What's the matter?

62

NORMAN. I'm afraid you're going to grab me and handcuff me to the steam pipe.

ANDY. (*Extends hand.*) Goodbye, Norman.

NORMAN. . . . Goodbye, Andy. (*Norman extends his hand to Andy, who in a flash of dexterity pulls up a pair of handcuffs from the pole table. One handcuff has been affixed to the steam pipe, the other one Andy puts on Norman's wrist. The handcuffs had been hidden by a pile of magazines. It happened so fast Norman is dumbfounded and can only stare blankly at what Andy has done. Andy rushes to remove the telephone from the pole table, puts it on the floor. He replaces the director's chair L. C., pulls back the round C. table and resets the chair R. of the table.*) . . . You dirty, no-good rat, I even have to write your lousy ideas! (*He pulls on the handcuffs.*)

ANDY. That one was my own, sweetheart. I heard you on the phone this morning with the A.P. Now we have one article to finish, one more page. And we're down to the finish line, Norman, because in forty-five minutes, Mr. Franklyn's two Neanderthal sons will be here to pick up our completed magazine or their six hundred dollars. And if I can't give them either one, I'll give them you.

NORMAN. (*Looks at him in disbelief.*) You mean you're serious? You actually intend, in real life, to keep a human being chained to a steam pipe?

ANDY. (*Goes R., gets typewriter from the sofa and takes it to the pole table.*) Until tomorrow—when the police find an unidentified broken object dangling from a post. (*Puts the typewriter on the table.*)

NORMAN. All right, Andy, I'm in no mood for the Prisoner of Zenda. Open up!

ANDY. Not until I see some paper work. (*Starts for the kitchen.*)

NORMAN. Where are you going?

ANDY. To the kitchen to get myself a tiny kumquat sandwich. (*He goes into the kitchen.*)

NORMAN. (*Shouts toward the window.*) Help! Help! I'm being held prisoner! (*He looks out the window and shouts to someone.*) Hey, lady! You wanna make a dollar? (*We hear a thunderous crash in the kitchen and a loud scream from Andy.*) What happened? (*From the kitchen, Andy staggers out holding his back in pain. He leans on the bar for support.*)

ANDY. Why did you wax the kitchen floor?

NORMAN. Are you crazy? I didn't wax the kitchen floor.

ANDY. (*Going toward* R. *chair.*) Well, the kitchen floor is waxed and if you didn't wax it, who did? (*The front door opens and Sophie enters carrying a package in tinfoil in one hand and a red suitcase in the other.*)

SOPHIE. (*Leaving the suitcase at the door.*) Ah've come to say goodbye. Ah froze a dozen fritters for you and be careful in the kitchen, ah just waxed the floor. (*Puts fritters on kitchen bar.*)

NORMAN. Sophie, he's gone crazy. Look what he's done to me. He's chained me to a steam pipe. (*Andy sits in* R. *chair.*)

SOPHIE. That won't be necessary anymore, Mr. Hobart. My bus is leavin' for Hunnicut in fifteen minutes. Since ah only put in a three-day week ah believe you have some money comin' back to you. (*She pours pennies out of her purse onto the* C. *table and starts out.*)

NORMAN. Sophie, you don't have to leave because of me. I'm not going to bother you anymore. I didn't even smell you coming in here.

SOPHIE. Ah'm glad, Norman. Ah'm not leavin' because of you. Ah don't blame you for the crazy way you been actin' lately. Ah understand it now. There are some things in life we just can't control. For no reason at all something strange and mystifyin' hits us and there's nothin' anybody can do about it except just sit and wait and hope it goes away just as fast as it came. Unfortunately ah don't see mine goin' away in the foreseeable future and that's why ah decided ah can't marry Lieutenant Burt Fenneman and that's why ah'm gettin' on the bus to Hunnicut an' ah can't say another word or else ah'll start cryin' all over this room. (*She starts to cry and runs toward the door. Picks up suitcase.*)

ANDY. Miss Rauschmeyer . . . wait! (*She stops at the door and waits.*) I am in great physical pain. I have a dislocated back from an overwaxed floor and a limp arm from a misguided Karate chop. (*Rises.*) But I just wanted you to know that I'm sorry . . . sorry that some of us react to certain stimuli . . . and that others of us don't. However, I have no wish to cause you any embarrassment or discomfort. Starting tomorrow I may be running this magazine myself. If you like, you can stay on—at half salary.

SOPHIE. (*Puts suitcase down outside door and returns to room.*) You expect me to stay here with me feelin' the way ah feel and you feelin' the way you don't? . . . Mr. Hobart, if ah wasn't afraid ah'd miss mah bus, ah'd really tell you somethin'. (*To Norman.*) Do yew have the time?

NORMAN. (*Looks at his watch.*) I don't even have a crystal.

SOPHIE. (*To Andy.*) Well, ah'll tell you anyway. You're right. Ah may be provincial and old-fashioned. Ah may believe in a lot of things like patriotism and the Constitution because that's the way ah was brought up, and that's the way ah feel. The trouble with you is you can't feel. You can't feel, you can't see, you can't hear and oh, boy, *you can't smell.* All you can do is think. But until you learn to use all those wonderful gadgets that nature has given you, you are only one-fifth of a man. Unfortunately by the time you get them all workin' and realize you are crazy about me, ah will be back home in mah high school gymnasium gettin' in shape for next year's Olympics. If you want mah advice, ah suggest you take those pennies and visit an eye, ear, nose and throat man. (*Starts for door.*) And maybe you ought to see a dentist too. Because mah former fiance, not happy with the recent turn of events, is on his way over here to separate your teeth from your face.

NORMAN. (*Jumps up and down happily.*) *Now* you're gonna get it! *Now* you'll first get it! (*Andy sits.*)

SOPHIE. Did you hear what ah said? There's an eight-foot Marine on his way here to comp you up!

NORMAN. (*Gleefully.*) You hear that? The Yanks are coming! It's all over now, brother. (*Yells out window.*) Come on, Leathernecks. (*He sings the "Marine Hymn."*) I'm glad I'm chained to a pipe because I wouldn't miss this for anything.

SOPHIE. (*Big smile.*) Ah wish ah could stay to see it.

ANDY. But you can't because you're leaving.

SOPHIE. (*Goes to stairs leading to front door.*) That's right, ah'm leavin'! Ah'm leavin'! Back to Hunnicut. And startin' tomorrow ah'm gonna swim a mile every day from now until next summer. (*Comes down steps toward c. table.*) Every American has to do what he does best for his country, and ah-can-swim! Ah'm gonna swim the United States right into a gold medal and this time ah'm gonna beat the livin' nose plugs offa that little fat girl from the desert. (*She picks the phone off the floor.*) I'm usin' your phone one more time. (*She dials.*) Gimme Western Union! (*To Andy.*) And what you did to blacken America's good name with your protestin' magazine, ah will whitewash with mah backstroke down in Mexico City. (*Into phone.*) Ah'd like to send a telegram, please. To Mr. Andrew Hobart, 217 Chestnut Hill, San Francisco. (*She looks at Andy.*) . . . Dear Mr. Hobart. Whether you like it or not, ah pledge allegiance to the flag of the United States of America . . . and to the Republic for which it stands, one nation, under God, indivisible, with Liberty and Justice for all . . . Sign that "A Patriot" and send it collect. (*She hangs up, puts the phone back on the floor and exits with a flourish.*)

NORMAN. You mean you're just going to sit there? She's going back to Hunnicut and you may never see her again!

ANDY. I'll see her again.

NORMAN. When?

ANDY. In 1972. I guarantee you she's the next President of the United States. Norman, I've had just about enough of you. Every man has his breaking point and my point just broke.

NORMAN. What are you gonna do?

ANDY. Murder! I'm going to commit cold-blooded murder right in this room. (*Rises and goes* L.) I'm going to kill the only thing in this world that really means anything to me—my magazine. (*He takes the key and unlocks Norman's handcuffs.*) There! Go on, you're free. Now get out of here and let me bury the body. (*He goes to the bulletin board while Norman goes* C. *Andy rips down the credo sign and breaks it over his knee.*) Maybe you were right. Maybe you were both right. Maybe I am crazy. Maybe it was lunatic to try to hold on to one tiny, not very important, insignificant little voice-in-the-wilderness against such overwhelming odds as a girl-smelling mental case and a wetback Martha Washington. (*Picks up magazines from pole table and takes them* R. *to the duffle bag on the sofa. Puts magazines into bag.*) I'm sure she'll be very happy now. America is safe tonight. In tribute, tomorrow Howard Johnson's will add another flavor. (*Throws duffle bag on floor.*) She's won, don't you see that, she's won. Divide and conquer, that's the way they do it. Well, we're divided and we're conquered. The war is over and we've surrendered. In reparations, she gets the Polish corridor, the free city of Danzig, three outfielders, two turtle doves and a partridge in a pear tree. (*He collapses into chair* R. *of table.*)

NORMAN. Well . . . we can't always have what we want.

ANDY. Go on, you were in such a hurry to go, why don't you go?

NORMAN. (*Goes* U. C. *to suitcase.*) Yeah . . . Want me to help you straighten up before I go?

ANDY. I wouldn't want you to be late for your appointment.

NORMAN. (*Nods. Picks up suitcase.*) One thing you were right about. Physical attraction isn't enough. It's like chewing gum. It starts off great, but the flavor doesn't last long.

ANDY. That's why they put five sticks in a pack. I'll see you, Norman. (*Rises and goes up steps to landing.*)

NORMAN. . . . Any idea what you're gonna do now?

ANDY. I might go back to Philadelphia. Maybe work for my father.

NORMAN. I can't picture you in your father's business.

ANDY. I don't know. There's a lot of important work being done in the kitchen cabinet field today.

NORMAN. Yeah. They say Formica is the hope of the future. (*Pause.*) I just want to say that if you decide not to go back to Philadelphia, that maybe someday, I don't know when, I'll be able to forget our differences, forget what's happened here the last few days, forget everything . . . And when I do, maybe someday I'll be back.

ANDY. I hope so, Norman . . . So long. (*Norman nods and leaves. There is a moment's silence, then the door opens and Norman returns.*)

NORMAN. I forgot everything; I'm back.

ANDY. What took you so long?

NORMAN. (*Puts suitcase down near kitchen bar.*) I got stuck in traffic. (*Andy comes down steps.*) Hey, tell the truth! Were you really going back to Philadelphia?

ANDY. Of course not. I was going to marry Mrs. Mackininee and open up the only Discotheque Funeral Parlor in California. (*They break up laughing.*)

NORMAN. And you'll be glad to know I'm Norman again. Norman the writer . . . (*Picks up typewriter from pole table.*) Norman, the man who's dedicated to this magazine. (*He goes* U. *to the* L. *window.*)

ANDY. (*Closing door.*) And promise me you'll never go off the deep end over a girl like that again.

NORMAN. (*At window.*) I'll promise tomorrow.

ANDY. Why not today?

NORMAN. 'Cause there's a gorgeous redhead across the street. (*Yells out.*) Hey, beautiful redhead lady, I love you!

ANDY. Norman, get back to that typewriter. (*Picks up phone and puts it on desk.*) We've got a magazine to get out.

NORMAN. (*Going to desk. Sits.*) All right. All right.

ANDY. And promise me you won't get up from that chair until you finish. (*Picks up dummy magazine from desk.*)

NORMAN. My fingers are glued to the keys.

ANDY. No distractions?

NORMAN. No distractions.

ANDY. (*Going* R.) No matter how much the smell in here is driving you crazy?

NORMAN. What smell?

ANDY. What do you mean, what smell? Her smell. Sophie.

NORMAN. I don't smell Sophie.

ANDY. Are you crazy? How can you not smell it? It's all over the room.

NORMAN. This room?

ANDY. Of course this room. She was just in here, wasn't she? I know the difference between a room smell and a Sophie smell and this is definitely . . . (*Drops dummy magazine on* C. *table.*) My God, what has happened to me?

NORMAN. You want me to chain you to the steam pipe?

ANDY. It's not possible. These things don't happen to me. You were second in your class in Dartmouth, *but I was first.*

NORMAN. It's just physical attraction. That's not for us. It's for hippopotamuses.

ANDY. I know that, damnit.

NORMAN. What are you screaming for?

ANDY. Because I'm standing here talking to you, and my hippopotamus is getting on the bus. (*Rushes* R. *to window on landing.*) Sophie! Sophie! (*The door flings open and Sophie rushes in.*)

SOPHIE. Ah been standin' out there just prayin' you'd say mah name. If you didn't say it in two more minutes, ah was gonna come back in here and say it for you.

ANDY. (*Comes down stairs.*) You didn't get on the bus.

SOPHIE. Ah didn't get on the bus because ah'm not goin' anywhere. Ah heard everything you said and if you were gonna give up this subversive magazine ah was personally gonna come in

68

here and tear you apart mahself. (*Comes down one step.*) Ah may not agree with what you say, but if you stop sayin' it, then no one will disagree and that is not the idea of democracy. (*Down one more step.*) We got free speech in this country and ah'm here to see that it stays free and spoken.

ANDY. You really didn't get on the bus.

SOPHIE. (*Goes R. to Andy.*) Of course ah didn't get on the bus. 'Cause in the first place ah'm crazy about you and in the second place ah left mah bus fare on your table.

ANDY. If you had gone back to Hunnicut, I'd have done something crazy like going after you on the next bus or the next train or the next plane or the next ship out of here. (*The telephone rings. Norman, at the desk, picks it up.*)

NORMAN. (*Into phone.*) Thomas Cook Travel Agency . . . No, it's his friend, Norman.

SOPHIE. Besides, ah got a job here that pays me seventy-five dollars a week and ah'm not about to give it up.

ANDY. Seventy-two dollars. We've got to stick to the President's guide lines.

SOPHIE. That's fine with me.

NORMAN. (*On phone.*) That sounds wonderful. I'll be right there. (*Hangs up and starts for the door.*)

SOPHIE. Where are you goin'?

NORMAN. Sky diving with Mrs. Mackininee.

SOPHIE. (*Few steps L. to Norman.*) You stay where you are and get back to work. We have a magazine to get out here. (*To Andy.*) Right? (*Norman sits again.*)

ANDY. Right! Only let me give you fair warning. It's not going to be easy. You start at eight and quit at seven.

SOPHIE. That's fine with me!

ANDY. I want pencils sharpened and papers stacked.

SOPHIE. That's fine with me!

ANDY. I want the books dusted, the floors cleaned and when I say hot coffee I mean hot coffee!

SOPHIE. That's fine with me!

ANDY. Good. Now that you know what the rules are . . . (*Goes to Norman who is sitting at the desk.*) Let's you and I get back to ripping apart the degenerating American way of life. Right? (*Sophie follows.*)

NORMAN. Right!

ANDY. (*Turns to Sophie.*) And if you've got anything to say, say it to yourself . . . Okay! Now that we all understand each other, maybe we'll finally get a little work done around here. (*Both Andy and Sophie smell each other. Andy crosses D. of her, goes to the chair R. of the C. table and sits. He picks up clipboard and goes to work. Norman starts typing. Sophie takes off her jacket and puts it on the back of the director's chair. She goes to the kitchen bar for the feather duster. As she starts dusting, she starts singing.*)

SOPHIE.

Mine eyes have seen the glory of the coming of the Lord;

(*She dusts U. L. table and pole table.*)

He is trampling out the vintage where the grapes of wrath are
stored,

(*From the wings—no, from the heavens, we hear voices joining Sophie in the stirring, building strains of this, the most inspiring of all patriotic hymns.*)

He hath loosed the fateful lightning of His terrible swift sword;
His truth is marching on.

CURTAIN

(*The curtain goes back up immediately. Sophie is busy dusting and singing. Both Andy and Norman look front incredulously. The curtain falls. Music runs out during curtain calls.*)

Glory! Glory! Hallelujah!

Glory! Glory! Hallelujah!

Glory! Glory! Hallelujah!

His truth goes marching on.

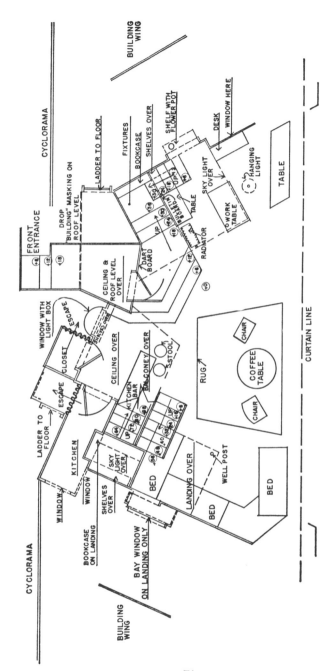

SCENE DESIGN

"THE STAR-SPANGLED GIRL"

71

PROPERTY PLOT

ON STAGE:

Sofa—D. R.—parallel with footlights

Table—R. of sofa—with magazines, books, gooseneck lamp, ash tray, dumbbell, empty cookie box, old alarm clock

Sofa—follows R. wall U.—with four pillows

Shelf—on R. wall above sofa—with 3 milk bottles of pennies, magazines, books

Bulletin board—above shelf—with pictures and clippings from newspapers and magazines

Sofa—under landing and stairs, at right angle with wall sofa—with newspapers, pillows

Rattan stool—onstage end of U. sofa—with tied bundle of newspapers —beer can, top of bundle

Wooden bar stool—U. of stairs leading to landing and D. of kitchen bar

On top of kitchen bar: (from R. to onstage end)
apothecary jar with candy, pot of ivy, ukulele, lamp, tall vase with feather duster

Top kitchen bar shelf:
R. section: books
on stage section: five glasses, empty whiskey bottles, beer can, two colored bottles

Middle kitchen bar shelf:
R. section: books
On stage section: books, magazines, carafe

Bottom kitchen bar shelf:
R. section: books
On stage section: bowl of fruit, beer can, magazines

In closet:
On back of door: bathrobe
On hooks on closet walls: vacuum cleaner hose, blue jacket on wooden hanger, tan jacket on wooden hanger, four other wooden hangers with pants, jackets, etc.
Broom, ironing board

Shelves—on wall L. of closet door

Top shelf: books, double glass cruet, copper watering can
Middle shelf: pipe rack with pipes, books, figurine
Bottom shelf: glass dish with fruit, metal box, miniature yard of ale

In kitchen—L. of closet door

  On u. wall: towel rack with towel, wall can opener, aluminum pan, aluminum skillet, electric kitchen clock, calendar, shelf with box of potato chips, two cans of vegetables

Wall switch—on wall—R. of c. door

Chain lock—on c. door

c. door—closed at top of show

In hall—u. c. of c. door

  Table with glass ash tray, mosaic ash tray

  Light fixture with 2 bulbs, and lamp shades

Light fixture—on wall, L. of c. door—with one light bulb

Bookcase—u. L., above bulletin board—with 7 shelves filled with books

Bulletin board—u. L.—with clothes hook with necktie—onstage end; wooden hanger with blue jacket—u. side of board, onstage end; clippings and pictures from newspapers and magazines

Small table—below bulletin board—with empty beer cans, stapler, stack of yellow paper, empty apothecary jar, mug with black pencils, clipboard with pencil on string, gummed labels, yellow printed pages

Under small table, on floor: tied bundle of old vouchers and bills, can of green paint, open—with stirrer, paint brush

Small radiator—onstage end of small table—with board on top for: scissors, electric pencil sharpener

D. of radiator, on floor: tied bundle of newspapers, cardboard carton, top of papers with files, paper

Small wooden stool—onstage of radiator

High wooden stool—L. of small table

Window—on L. wall—with match-stick blinds, window closed at top of show

Mat—on floor, outside window

Large magazine picture and article pasted on cardboard—on wall under window

Slant-top desk—D. of window—with *Time* magazine, unabridged dictionary—open, pipe

  In D. drawer: small cereal box with 3 corn flakes

Magazine pictures pasted on cardboard—on wall, under slant-top desk

Miscellaneous pictures and papers—on desk rung

Bulletin board—on wall above slant-top desk—with mirror, necktie, sign "A Remedy for a Sick Society," pictures, clippings

Narrow pole table—L. c.—with phone with push buttons, pile of *Time* magazines—near pole

Under pole table—on floor: tied bundle of old vouchers, bills, etc., stack of *Time* magazines

Desk—D. L., parallel with footlights

On top: (from onstage to L.)

Rubber cement, tape recorder turned on with microphone, tape evenly divided

Dummy magazine with paper clip holding loose pieces of typed yellow pages on top

Manuscript with paper clip

Portable typewriter with yellow paper in it, newspaper clippings with large paper clip, stack of yellow paper

Stack of long white addressed envelopes, roll of stamps

Gooseneck lamp, erasers, bell

Onstage side of table:

Clipboard hanging on hook—with: bills, papers

Pile of magazines—on floor under L. end of desk with: several *Fallout* magazines—on top

Chair—U. of desk

Worklight with green shade—hanging over desk

Wastebasket—onstage end of desk with: bills, one unopened envelope

Phone cord is attached to U. C. desk leg

Rug—painted on ground cloth

C. table—with: stamp pad, rubber stamp, tin ash tray, coffee pot, one newspaper, three magazines

Plate with: crumbs, dabs of jam

Empty jam jar—no top, mug with: black pencils, yellow pencils, coffee cup

Director's chair—L. of C. table

Captain's chair—R. of C. table

Telescope—on landing

Blue and yellow necktie—R. landing post

Light fixture—on landing wall, D. of window—with 2 bulbs

Window—on R. landing wall—open at top of show

Two bookshelves—on landing R. wall—with: books, pot of ivy

Built-in bookcase—U. wall on landing—with: books, vase, apothecary jar with candy, tin box

Built-in bookcase—on balcony wall parallel with footlights—with: books, statue, pot of ivy

Andy's door—on balcony—closed at top of show

Norman's door—on balcony—closed at top of show

OFF STAGE:

On roof:

Basket of clothes including blue shirt—1-1

Men's socks

Norman's bedroom:

    Bon voyage basket—Norman—1-2
    Stack of books—Norman—3
    Flower box with plants—Norman—3
    Einstein photo—Norman—3

Kitchen:

    Damp mop—Norman—1-2
    Dish cloth—Sophie—2-2
    Bowl with: mixing spoon, flour—Sophie—2-2
    Sauce pan—Sophie—2-2
    Frying pan with: fritter, spatula—Sophie—2-2
    Asbestos glove—Sophie—2-2

Off u. c.:

    Fruitcake on plate—Sophie—1-1
    2 briefcases—Andy—1-1 and 1-2
    Blue paper bag with: bill (taped to one side at top)
       Jar of watermelons
       Tin of herring   } in brown bag
       Jar of kumquats
       Jar of brandied peaches
       8 other small grocery items—Norman—1-2
    ½ apple—Andy—2-1
    Small flight bag—Andy—2-1
    Towel with bathing suit—Andy—2-1
    Terry cloth robe—Andy—2-1
    Noxzema jar—Andy—2-1
    YWCA bag—Sophie—2-1
    Fallout magazine—Sophie—2-1
    Bottle of wine in paper bag—Norman—2-2
    Pennies in white shoulder bag—Sophie—3
    Red suitcase—Sophie—3
    Package of fritters in foil—Sophie—3
Crash equipment—off stage, between closet and hall—u. R. C.

Personal Props:

    Watch—Andy
    Watch—Norman

END OF ACT ONE

Clean up
   Bills from waste basket

Strike:
   Dumbbell from D. R. table to off
   Stack of newspapers and beer can from rattan stool to off
   Attache case from under desk to off
   Attache case from U. of bulletin board to off
   Grocery bag from U. kitchen bar to off
   Pipe from kitchen back to slant-top desk
   From pole table:
      Bon voyage basket to off
      Glue to radiator
      Dummy magazine to desk
   From C. table:
      Coffee pot to off
      Coffee cup to off
   From desk:
      Clippings to off
      Gooseneck lamp to off
      Tape recorder to Norman's room
   From U. L. table:
      Ukulele back to kitchen bar
      Apothecary jar to off

Set:
   On slant-top desk:
   2 hair brushes, electric cordless razor
   On C. table:
      Ash tray with torn paper
      Fallout magazine
      Mug with pencils to D. of table
   Coffee can—C. of D. sofa
   Yellow paper and two paper cups—on rattan stool
   C. door—ajar
   Both upstairs doors—closed
   L. window—open

END OF ACT TWO SCENE ONE

Strike:
   From D. R. sofa:
      Small flight bag to off
      Towel with bathing suit to off

76

Coffee can of pennies to off
Terry cloth robe to off
From c. table:
  Clipboard to off
  Crumpled paper to off
From desk:
  Noxzema to off
  Crumpled paper from floor to off
YWCA bag from pole table to off
3 milk bottles of pennies from Sophie to off

Set:
  On desk:
  Manuscript, bell on manuscript
  On c. table:
  Fallout magazine
  Sports Illustrated magazine
  Plate
  Knife
  Fork
  Napkin—under fork
  Stack of books on D. R. shelf above sofa
  Director's chair—face R.

END OF ACT TWO SCENE TWO

Strike:
  From c. table:
  Plate with fritter to off
  Silverware to off
  Napkin to off
  Sports Illustrated to off
  Fallout magazine to stack under desk
  From slant-top desk:
  Electric razor to off
  Hairbrushes to off
  Envelopes with stamps from desk to off
  Manuscript from D. sofa to off
  Vacuum hose from U. kitchen bar to closet

Set:
  On desk:
  Tape recorder moved to c. marks, P.A. setting (4) and plug
    recorder in; dummy magazine, stack of yellow paper

On kitchen bar:
   Feather duster in vase, 8-pack of empty coke bottles (u. of bar
      on floor)
On sofa:
   Duffle bag, typewriter with yellow paper
On pole table:
   Handcuffs (under magazines), telephone (facing u.)
Suitcase—open—L. of stairs—on floor
u. L. table—stack of yellow paper
On c. table—clipboard
Andy's bedroom door closed
Norman's bedroom door open
c. door—closed

COSTUMES

ANDY

Act One Scene One

   Tan slacks
   Tan jacket
   Red, white and blue, check shirt
   Black knit tie
   Gray socks
   Desert suede shoes
   Blue blazer
   Yellow and blue striped tie

Act One Scene Two:

   Same as above except: no tie no blue blazer, brown loafers

Act Two Scene One:

   Same tan slacks
   Purple sweat shirt
   Plaid cotton jacket with hood
   Tan socks
   Same desert suede shoes

Act Two Scene Two:

   Same tan slacks
   Same tan socks
   Same suede shoes
   Same plaid jacket
   Yellow long sleeve shirt
   White long sleeve sweater

Act Three

   Same tan slacks
   Same tan socks
   Same suede shoes
   Blue wool sports shirt over red and white long sleeve shirt
   Light tan raincoat

SOPHIE

Act One Scene One:

   Yellow wool dress with daisy
   Yellow bracelet
   Yellow medium-heel shoes

Act One Scene Two:

Pink wool skirt
White long sleeve blouse
Pink, green and white plaid jacket with **daisy**
Beige medium-heel shoes
White gloves in jacket pocket

Act Two Scene One:

YWCA blue bathing suit
Man's light blue long-sleeve shirt
White denim pants
White sneakers
White sailor's hat
Dance tights
Whistle on a chain

Act Two Scene Two:

Coral dress with daisy
Blue and white striped apron
Same beige shoes
Same dance tights

Act Three:

White wool skirt
Navy blazer with Olympic emblem
White shell blouse
Same beige shoes
White shoulder-strap purse

NORMAN

Act One Scene One:

Dark green slacks
Peach long sleeve shirt
Tan cardigan sweater
Gray socks
Black loafers

Act One Scene Two

Same green slacks
Same shirt
Red sneakers
Light olive corduroy jacket

Act Two Scene One
Tan corduroy slacks
Blue long sleeve shirt
Brown shoes
Same socks
Same corduroy jacket
White handkerchief

Act Two Scene Two:
White terry-cloth short sleeve shirt
Same corduroy slacks
Same socks
Same brown shoes

Act Three:
Tan suit
Red, white and blue check shirt
Maroon tie
Same socks
Same brown shoes

NEW
PLAYS

THE AFRICAN COMPANY PRESENTS
RICHARD III
by Carlyle Brown

EDWARD ALBEE'S
FRAGMENTS and THE MARRIAGE PLAY

IMAGINARY LIFE
by Peter Parnell

MIXED EMOTIONS
by Richard Baer

THE SWAN
by Elizabeth Egloff

Write for information as to
availability
DRAMATISTS PLAY SERVICE, Inc.
440 Park Avenue South   New York, N.Y. 10016

NEW
PLAYS

THE LIGHTS
by Howard Korder

THE TRIUMPH OF LOVE
by James Magruder

LATER LIFE
by A.R. Gurney

THE LOMAN FAMILY PICNIC
by Donald Margulies

A PERFECT GANESH
by Terrence McNally

SPAIN
by Romulus Linney

*Write for information as to
availability*
DRAMATISTS PLAY SERVICE, Inc.
440 Park Avenue South   New York, N.Y. 10016

NEW
PLAYS

LONELY PLANET
by Steven Dietz

THE AMERICA PLAY
by Suzan-Lori Parks

THE FOURTH WALL
by A.R. Gurney

JULIE JOHNSON
by Wendy Hammond

FOUR DOGS AND A BONE
by John Patrick Shanley

DESDEMONA, A PLAY ABOUT A
HANDKERCHIEF
by Paula Vogel

*Write for information as to
availability*
DRAMATISTS PLAY SERVICE, Inc.
440 Park Avenue South   New York, N.Y. 10016